MW01075253

# SERVANT *of the* KING

MEMOIR OF MODERN APOSTLE KEMPER CRABB

CHANA KEEFER

Printed and bound in the USA

Cover design and interior layout | www.pearcreative.ca

ISBN: 978-0-9892197-2-3

# DEDICATION

This book is dedicated to the missionaries, martyrs, and servants of the Kingdom of Heaven whose names we have never heard, but whose lives echo throughout eternity.

# TABLE OF CONTENTS

# FOREWORD

All of this started happening when a coach retired.

But who is Kemper Crabb? Why is he so competent at this? What makes him tick? Why do people feel so drawn to him? Why do they do more for him than they would without him?

Kemper is an East Texas son of a tough and fun German mother and a reserved Coushatta Indian father. He took the contradictory qualities of their two nationalities and became a unique spirit. Like others born in the 1930s, he grew up poor and didn't know he was. He hunted in the piney woods for the family's dinner table, fished among water moccasins, raced with his friends through the forests, hurtling fences with poles for the sheer joy of it.

What's he like?

Kemper loves to laugh and wants others to be entertained. He remembers all the jokes he heard in junior high and never hesitates to review them for everyone, no matter how many complaints. Groans only fuel the humor engine.

He likes being close. When his children were young, a trip to buy bread was a great opportunity to throw both kids in the car to go with him. He says the concept of spending "quality time" is rubbish. Spend ordinary time, all the time.

He keeps up with friends and students. All his friends know he might show up on their doorstep at any given time. All his students know he will remember their name and the nickname he bestowed should they cross paths in the grocery aisle or at a commencement address he is giving.

Things work for Kemper. He speaks to things and to people. A broken down motorcycle will start after he has spoken to it. When something temporarily doesn't work around him, he is momentarily surprised. He expects things to work. And they do. It often seems he is doing nothing overt, but things are magically happening wherever he is.

Kemper is hard on minor errors but supportive on big mistakes. He delights in weaving tales of the "Snap Dragon" that lurks in the attic for his grandchildren, or suddenly baring his teeth like a growling lion and scattering a gaggle of African children who shriek with laughter and come back for more.

He is courageous. No matter how many times he is put in prison for "altering karma" by introducing children and lepers to Christianity, he returns. His body bears up under the brutality but reminds him daily with the pain in his shoulders and his heart.

He loves passionately. He loves his Lord and is reading His Word in every silent moment. From cover to cover, his Bible has been studied many times every year for many years. He doesn't endlessly quote the chapter and the verse, though it's certain they are stored in his faultless memory. He reads to learn and love again each word.

He loves continuously. He prays for people who don't pray—and who will never know he prays for them.

He loves stray animals and carries a can of dog food in his truck, "just in case."

He loves easygoing, positive times but will join a fight—and will win.

He's entrepreneurial and loves things that move. When he was thirteen, he was licensed to drive an eighteen-wheeler. While he was coaching, he ran a canoe rental business on the Guadalupe River. Many people could have lived on the profits he made on the fifty-plus motorcycles he bought, rode hard, and sold over the years.

He seems tireless and always sees in his mind the next 100 places to go and things to do. Amazingly, he acts on these visions, while others dream on.

But he hates squash.

*By Martha White,*
*Servants of the King Board Member & Historian 1995-2005*

MARTHA WHITE (R) & UGANDAN HOME BASE DIRECTOR, PROSSY ISABIRYE

The man drew no attention to himself in the crowd filing toward the waiting airplane. Clothed in blue jeans and collared shirt, no one would think he had been imprisoned multiple times, held hundreds of dying children in his arms or worked side-by-side with Mother Teresa. He was simply an aging man with a kind smile and alert expression. He was overlooked by all—except the one who stood at the door of the terminal, another who was ignored by the crowd—because no one else could see him.

The messenger's words were concise:

"Heavenly servant, it is time to tell your story."

# Chapter One

## THE SERVANT

**"Is not this the kind of fasting I have chosen: to loose the chains of injustice and untie the cords of the yoke, to set the oppressed free and break every yoke?"**

**(Isaiah 58:6)**

Angry, armed soldiers poured into the courtyard where a group of young children, several orphanage workers and one white-skinned American missionary gathered.

"You must pay for the children you stole!" the leader of the armed men demanded.

"No," the missionary replied. "You know we cannot do this. If I pay you for these children we rescued, you will report that we are buying human flesh. If I pay you, you will always come back for more."

"You will pay me," the soldier's voice rose, "or I will kill them."

"No," the missionary replied again, "I cannot."

The soldier nodded toward the nearest child. His second-in-command grabbed the child by the arm.

"No!" A young voice broke the tense moment as a sickly child stumbled toward the missionary. This was one of the children the missionary and his helpers had found during the night, tied to a post in a back alley, waiting alone to die in order to "improve his Karma in the next reincarnation."

"Let them kill me," the child insisted, plucking at the missionary's sleeve. "I'm going to die anyway. Tell them to kill me instead."

The soldier who held the other child looked to his commander for direction. The leader gave a curt nod. With one swing of his sword, the soldier lopped off the sickly child's head.

A stunned silence followed as all stared at the horror of the small, decapitated body.

"You will pay me!" the commander demanded again.

The missionary lifted his tear-filled eyes. He saw what the others in that courtyard could not see. Angels. A battalion of heavenly hosts closed in around the soldiers.

"No," he answered again.

The commander yanked his head toward his second-in-command once more, indicating another kill, but the second soldier's eyes were wide, filled with fear. "I cannot," he replied.

Without a word, the commander pulled his gun and shot the fearful soldier.

In that moment, the heavenly forces moved in, still invisible to all but the missionary. The soldiers looked 'round for a panic-filled split second, then fled, leaving only the leader behind. With a look of fear toward the missionary, the commander also hurried away.

The missionary, though overawed by the presence of heavenly hosts, wept as he, the children, and orphanage workers tended to the corpses at their feet, praying over the child and the soldier and burying them with dignity.

Though the victory was hard-won and the missionary still recounts the story with tears, the soldiers never returned.

---

Who is this man?

He is known by many names on his mission ventures. In Africa he is called Simba, meaning "lion" or the longer version, "Empologoma Mwana wa Katonda," which is Swahili for "Lion of God." In India, he is called "Talh Singh," which has the same meaning as his African moniker. He has embraced these nicknames in order to accomplish God's directives without calling attention to himself. He wants all glory given where it belongs—to the One he serves. To family and friends he is Kemper Crabb, a servant of God who operates with bold spiritual authority, accomplishing tasks that seem more suited to the fictional Indiana Jones than to a native Texan, who simply purposed to fulfill Christ's great commission to go into all the world, teach the good news of salvation, and alleviate suffering. He delves into the dark depths of spiritual depravity, overcoming forces of evil through simple obedience to God. Through his ministry, whole families, villages and even local cultures are transformed and freed from spiritual slavery.

Some mindboggling facts:

1. The number of those who have professed faith in Christ in Kemper's 30-plus years of mission excursions—at last count, more than 11 million.

2. The number of schools built under his direction—400 and counting.

3. The number of churches built and inaugurated to serve the local communities in India, Africa and China—more than 1800.

Those he serves, and those who have accompanied him into some of the most dangerous areas of the world, where local authorities are most hostile to the message of Christ, have reported miraculous healings, demoniacs released, and even several people raised from the dead.[1]

If true, why have we not heard of this modern Apostle Paul?

What circumstances would fashion such a bold leader?

How is he able to accomplish the seemingly impossible?

What motivates Kemper to continue his work without notoriety, with constant danger, and at great personal expense?

As with all good stories, the best place to start is at the beginning.

1 Kemper recalls 17 resurrections

# Chapter Two
## HEAVENLY MUSIC

**It costs nothing to come to Jesus.**

**It costs a lot to follow Him.**

**It costs everything to serve Him.**

**~Kemper Crabb**

**1938**

The child tossed and turned on the bed as his temperature soared higher. 102, 103, 104. When the thermometer read 105 degrees, the doctor tried to prepare the family. "If he survives, he will have permanent brain damage. He will probably never walk or talk. He will be in a vegetative state."

But still the scarlet fever burned, raising the temperature ever higher.

106, 107.

The boy's skin blistered and began to slough off as he writhed on the bed.

Then it happened.

As the doctor's mournful words droned on and the pain became even more unbearable, the boy who waited to die heard music. It was more beautiful than anything he had heard in his six short years of life. Then, in the music, he heard a voice. In his simple, child's mind he never questioned. This was the voice of God.

> "Child, you could go on and exit this life and everything would be fine. Or, you could fight and live and I will always be with you."

Through his pain, the child chose the path of more pain. He chose to live.

The next day, the fever had receded and the boy began to recover at record speed. It was a hard road. He had to learn to speak again. Everyday tasks were difficult or assisted, but he continued to improve and, to the astonishment of doctors and family alike, he surpassed former plateaus. He was smarter, his speech was back to normal and, when his parents could afford the surgery, his clubbed feet were corrected, further opening this former sickly child's world. Not only could he run, he could run faster than most. Not only could he talk and reason, he became a leader in his school—student body president, in fact.

And every time something good happened, a new honor, award or touchdown, the boy heard the beautiful, heavenly music once more. But he kept this fact to himself.

So young Kemper Crabb—born club-footed and almost deaf, a German/Jew/Coushata Indian in East Texas where his lineage made him an outcast, who barely survived a fierce bout of Scarlet Fever—grew strong as he ran and played. His hearing improved too. In fact, he could still hear what no one else could; the heavenly music that played with celebration for each of his victories. Kemper, the child who had been at death's door, began to live, really live; fearless, joyful, a natural leader. And he sought to learn more about this God who had saved him from the brink of death.

---

How does a child live who realizes he's alive and healthy due to a miracle?

With joy.

Kemper began to play sports with reckless abandon, excelling at all he tried. He ran faster, played harder and enjoyed the relative stardom of small town Texas athletics. He exhibited fearlessness in business pursuits by acquiring his license to drive an eighteen-wheeler at the ripe old age of thirteen. His fearlessness even turned to thrill seeking when he began to ride bulls at local rodeos. Riding bulls was an exciting outlet. Kemper was good at it, he won a lot, and he enjoyed the attention from young ladies who gathered to admire his feats. When the time came for higher learning, he received athletic scholarships from Sam Houston State University where he continued his notoriety as a star football player.

KEMPER EXCELLED IN HIGH SCHOOL SPORTS

Kemper received his Bachelor of Science degree in physical education in 1954 and his Master of Science degree in education three years later, both from Sam Houston State.

Was he perfect? Not according to college faculty members who advised his future wife not to marry him. "He's dated everyone in town! Plus he's a truck driver. That's as bad as a traveling salesman!" they warned her.

In his own defense when recalling the situation, Kemper teases, "It was a *really* small town." By modern standards, his escapades were harmless enough. The large belt buckles he won as prizes for bull riding he gave to one of his many admirers. He admits to some bar fights and partying with his fraternity brothers. Luckily for Tommye Crabb, Kemper's naysayers were proven wrong. Six decades of marriage later, he still calls her "Sweetie" and she still calls him "Babe."

KEMPER & TOMMYE ON THEIR WEDDING DAY

## Mystery of the Kingdom #1

The spoken word:

You have the authority of the entity (or the One) you represent.

As a young man, Kemper had a natural ability to influence people but knew this too was a gift since true authority came from God, the One whom he represented. This viewpoint left no room for ego. The authority was to be used for building the Kingdom of Heaven, not for selfish pursuits. He played football at Sam Houston State where his team won Conference. The New York Giants even tapped him as a late-term draft choice. "I told them (New York Giants representatives) I looked good due to the skill of the players around me. They thought it was some kind of faux-humility, but it really was all about the linemen who defended me. Seriously. One of them weighed, like, a gazillion pounds. They were *really* good."

Kemper relates the end of his professional football opportunities. "I may have been a late-term draft choice for the Giants, but I was a first-round draft pick for Uncle Sam." So, rather than a professional football career, Kemper joined the armed forces in 1954 and ended up serving two years during the Korean conflict. Tommye, his new bride, joined Kemper where he was stationed in Panama.

First-Round Draft Pick for Uncle Sam

But football opportunities and military service aside, when asked what he planned for the future, Kemper would answer without hesitation, "I will be a coach and a missionary."

# Chapter Three
## THE CALL

**The things you act on from this book are what you believe. The rest is just empty religious talk.**

**~Peter Lord, on the Bible**

True to his word, Kemper was a coach at Huntsville High, where he led his team to a state championship. In all, Kemper spent 30 years in education as a coach, athletic director, and professor of kinesiology. But he never forgot his other ambition. In the midst of his most demanding family and coaching years, an encounter with an evangelist at their home church further strengthened his resolve to lay all on the line for God's purpose.

The year was 1969. Kemper and his family attended a revival at his church where Peter Lord, an evangelist from Florida, delivered a no-compromise message. Kemper, his family, and several of his friends would never be the same.

"Peter told us about the importance of covenants* with God, and about choosing to be 'unoffended' so unforgiveness could never separate us from The Father. So my family and I made a covenant together to remain unoffended. Ya just don't hold onto offenses in the first place."[2]

But Peter Lord had more to say to this typical Southern Baptist congregation. Fixing them with his steely gaze, he lifted up a Bible for all to see. "The things you act on from this book are what you believe. The rest is just empty religious talk."

"Oh. My. Gosh," Kemper exclaims as he recalls the moment. "That changed everything."

Kemper and a few of his friends who responded to that mandate met together and decided to put their beliefs into action. They were no longer satisfied to just talk about the millions of people around the world who had never heard the gospel message and who suffered from the lack of basic necessities. It was time for action.

Kemper was still coaching, very successfully in fact. He even led several students on his team to Christ. But during school holidays, he sought ways to obey Jesus' command to "go into all the world." Therefore this former bull-rider, star athlete and championship coach dove into the deep waters of foreign missions. But he didn't feel God calling him to just any mission work. As stated before, Kemper sought out the darkest, most hopeless, notoriously dangerous situations. "After all," he reasoned, "Jesus went to the sick, those who needed him the most. I'm just called to do what He did."

For Kemper, the formula was and is simple.

1. Ask for God's guidance

2. Hear God's direction

3. Do it.

"I would go to White's Chapel in London, to the Underground in Vienna, to the sewer district in Paris, or Amsterdam's Red Light District."

2 One of the Mysteries of the Kingdom. More on covenants in Chapter 5

On these uncharted excursions, supernatural intervention was necessary.

"Sure there were times I was scared," Kemper admits. "You'd have to be crazy to not feel some fear in those places. But I knew God was with me and He loved those people. That gives *a Boldness*. Plus, I knew I had the authority of the One I represent." [3]

During one Christmas break, Kemper went to Paris. God had given him direction to go to the sewer district and spread the gospel. Only problem was, he didn't know where to find the entrance to the sewer district. How was he to preach to the outcasts living underground? He walked around downtown Paris one night, praying God would lead him. He saw an old woman carrying a big bag of groceries. He asked her, "May I help you with that, ma'am?" She ignored him. He tried again, "In the name of my Savior and Lord Jesus, may I help you with that?" She responded in English that he was a kind young man and handed him the bag.

When he carried the groceries to her house, she invited him in. She asked him what he was doing in town and he said that, though it might sound crazy, he was intending somehow to spread the gospel down in the sewers. With tears in her eyes and without saying a word, the woman walked over to what looked like a cabinet on the other side of the room. She opened it. Inside was a spiral staircase leading down to the sewers.

The woman introduced Kemper to groups of people living there. He says they weren't bad people, more like misfits. He told them the gospel story and cast out some demons. They accepted the teaching about Jesus very readily and even embraced his teaching on casting out demons as well.

---

These excursions continued during summer and winter breaks until 1984, just about three years before retirement. Kemper's ministry was about to catapult toward a whole new level of commitment.

3 Mystery of the Kingdom #1

As Kemper prayed about where to go on his upcoming break, he received surprising direction. "As clear as day, God said, 'India.'" Kemper's immediate response was a teasing, "Couldn't we go somewhere a little nicer?"

He asked God for confirmation, like the biblical Gideon who tested God's guidance with the fleece. "About ten seconds later, I kid you not, one of my coworkers popped his head in and said, 'Kemper, let's go to India.'"

At the last moment, the other man was unable to go. Regardless, Kemper stuck with the plan, though he was alone and didn't know anyone in India.

But taking risks at God's direction had become a way of life for Kemper. Vishal Mangalwadi, noted Indian author and Christian philosopher,* agreed to meet with Kemper. When he arrived in New Delhi, India, there was a note from the revered author saying Mangalwadi would not be available for another 10 days. What to do in the meantime? Kemper decided to visit the Taj Mahal. While at the famous landmark, he overheard a conversation about snow skiing in India's mountainous region of Kashmir. The thrill seeker in him couldn't resist. "Lots of people have skied Vail. How many can say they've skied Kashmir?"

But for the first time in decades, there was no snow in the mountains of Kashmir, India. He rented a driver to show him around and asked to go to the downtown area. The driver responded, "No. It's too dangerous." But Kemper was determined. He had the driver drop him off in downtown Agra, truly one of the poorest places in the world. Kemper found himself surrounded by people staring in anger at a white guy infiltrating "their" district.

Kemper saw a child dying on the street. He went to the child and picked him up. Hindus surrounded him and drew their swords. They were very protective and did not want this white man to alter the karma of the child. Kemper obeyed the angry crowd and laid the child back down. Helplessly, he watched the child die.

Kemper on early trip to India

"I was angry at God and argued with Him," Kemper admits. "How could He allow such suffering?" But God granted the frustrated missionary a precious gift. "This was the first time I had a vision of Jesus. I could see the child sitting on His knee."

But those who suffered in that region of India were an overwhelming problem. "The orphans and lepers broke my heart. I thought, 'God, what in the world can I do about this?'"

### Mystery of the Kingdom #2

Much more can be accomplished by keeping a low profile.

(Let others take the credit.)

The determined Texas football coach returned to the nearby town of Srinagar with the dilemma of the poor and suffering foremost in his mind. In Srinagar were little shops where higher caste Hindus would sit and smoke very large pipes. Kemper approached a group of them. "Don't you see all these kids on the streets around here?" he asked. The men replied they couldn't do anything about it because they were under the authority of a warlord and couldn't question him. Kemper asked if there was some way he could speak with this warlord. The men set up a meeting.

So Kemper brought his concerns about the orphans to the district's ruling warlord. "I asked if he would help me build an orphanage for the children in his district since this would make him look good in the eyes of the people. 'You help me and I'll make sure you get the credit,'" Kemper assured him.

INDIA'S CHILDREN & ORPHANS BROKE KEMPER'S HEART

The warlord agreed.

Spurred by success, Kemper asked if there was some way to do the same thing in other poor mountainous districts around Kashmir. The warlord said, "No. The other districts are under rival warlords and we don't communicate if we can avoid it." Kemper asked to be introduced to the other warlords. The meeting was arranged. The others also agreed to help Kemper build orphanages in their area.

A few years later, after the orphanages were built, Kemper approached these same warlords. "It would be really useful," he told them, "if we could build a hospital or large clinic to serve the area." One of the warlords noted this ambitious endeavor could only be accomplished if the three combined their resources. Eventually, they did just that. They worked together to build a hospital. Through this process, they formed an alliance.

Years later when Kemper was in Calcutta, one of the revered Sikhs[4] told him, "You are the most honored man in Kashmir. You brought the warlords together and they resisted Pakistan."[5]

Kemper was dumbfounded by the man's regard. "Wow. Usually you have no idea what is truly accomplished by simply aiming to build the Kingdom of Heaven."

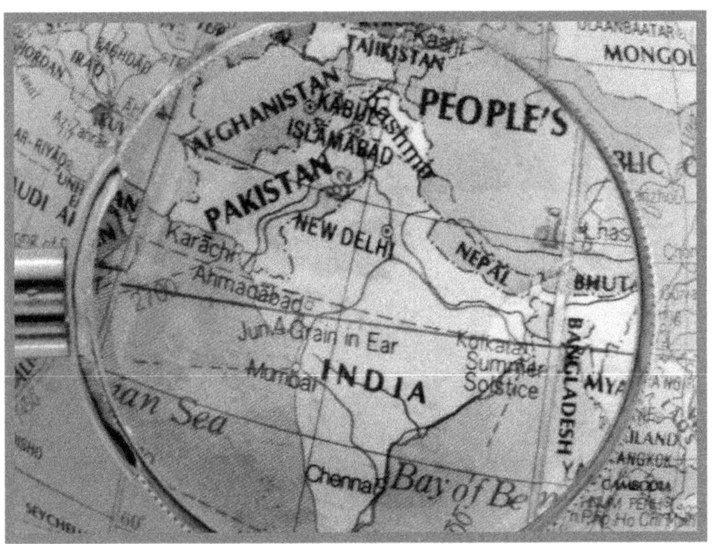


MAP SHOWING THE PAKISTANI/INDIAN BORDER AND THE KASHMIR DISTRICT.

Thus began Kemper's focus on India where he encountered sickness and suffering the likes of which he had not experienced before.

4 Holy men who believe in and worship one supreme, omnipotent God.

5 For more information regarding the Pakistani/Kashmir conflict go to: www.insightonconflict.org/conflicts/pakistan/conflict-profile/

But Kemper also had a family; a son and daughter, now grown, and his wife who had known life with her adventurous, no-holds-barred mate would be anything but boring. What did she think of Kemper's dangerous travels?

"I knew God was with him," says Tommye. She adds with a smile and roll of her eyes, "I also knew, Lord help anyone who got in the way of what God told him to do!"

So Kemper continued to reach out to the poorest, the most hopeless, the dying, and the outcasts, while his wife remained at home and prayed.

KEMPER ON A SHUTTLE FOR ONE OF THE SCHOOLS HE HELPED ESTABLISH IN INDIA

When Kemper sought ordination through the Baptist church to aid him in his burgeoning mission work, his request was rejected due to his age. Plus, the fact his wife was not called to go with him caused church officials to question Kemper's calling to the mission field as well. This is why, though he and Tommye have attended a Baptist church for decades, he ended up seeking ordination through the Episcopal denomination. "My son, (Kemper Jr.) is an ordained Episcopal priest. When he heard about the trouble I was having, he said, 'Dad, I'll see what I can do to help.'"

Thus Kemper began studying for his ordination under the Communion of Evangelical Episcopal Churches, which is under the authority of the Archbishop of Canterbury. He was ordained as an Episcopal priest in 1990.

KEMPER WAS ORDAINED IN 1990

"Early on," Kemper's wife Tommye admits, "I had a bit of a grudge toward God because I didn't feel called to the same path. Here I was with our newly empty nest just rattling around in our too-big house." She continued to teach as a college professor, but Kemper's long absences were difficult for her.

"For five years I was mad at God and mad at Kemper. I was just horrified. Kids were grown. It was hard. But I knew God hadn't called me to go with him."

Tommye did, however, discover a vital purpose in Kemper's ministry. "When I would sense he was in danger, I would call friends from our church and we would all pray." Later, sometimes years down the road,

Tommye would learn just how dangerous some of the situations Kemper survived really were, since he hesitated to reveal everything.

"I knew she was worried enough," Kemper says. "Plus, back in those days, there were only two phones in India and they were both broken," he jokes. "Seriously, it could be two full months before I would get the chance to talk to her and ya don't wanna share the bad stuff over the phone. Besides, there are some things you'd rather just forget. But I would often find out Tommye and our friends had been praying right at the time I needed it."

# Chapter Four
# HEAVENLY CO-WORKERS

**Forget not to show love unto strangers: for thereby some have entertained angels unawares.**

**-Hebrews 13:2 (ASV)**

Already Kemper could hear heavenly music no one else could hear, but as his mission adventures amped up a notch, his spiritual life also delved further into uncharted waters; at least uncommon in America's pragmatic society. Even in the church, this new realm was unusual.

He began to see and even communicate with God's messengers.

The first experience of a supernatural nature occurred at home when he was in prayer. He could see a frightening specter in the shape of a huge, dark wolf head barreling toward their Texas home. But this vision crossed into the natural realm when Kemper's house began to shake.

"It was so frightening and moving so fast I barely had time to rebuke it in Jesus' name. When I did, the vision passed over us with a *whoosh*."

When Kemper explained to a frightened Tommye what had made their house shake, she was fascinated. "You can keep the scary stuff," she said, "but I'd love to see an angel."

According to Kemper though, one doesn't get to pick and choose. When he has insight into the spiritual realm, it's not just the heavenly that is revealed, he perceives evil as well. Kemper shakes his head with a grim expression. "Ya don't wanna see that."

The next night, Tommye woke Kemper with a scream. At the foot of the bed stood an angel, tall, bright as lightning and awesome. "We were both so frightened we just froze and stared. After that," Kemper chuckles, "Tommye said she was just fine leaving the angel sightings to me."

Kemper's first experience of actually speaking with an angel occurred in India, on a highway that goes up toward Tibet. "I saw a young blind girl following a dog by holding to the dog's tail." Kemper says he could tell the dog was also blind because it was taking slow, high, careful steps. "I wanted to help so I headed toward them." But immediately, about a dozen armed Gurkhas[6] blocked his path.

"It's against the law to interfere with someone's Karma[7] and they weren't going to let me anywhere near her."

Kemper hated to give up, but an angel appeared to him with a message that put his heart at peace. "Heavenly servant, I will take care of the child *and* the dog."

The angel proceeded to instruct Kemper with some of the mysteries on which he has based his outreach ever since. "He said these were revealed

---

6 Gurkhas are indigenous people mainly from the mid-western, eastern Nepal and the Gorkhaland region of India. Their name derives from the 8th century Hindu term "Gorakhnath" which means "warrior-saint Guru."

7 In the Hindu religion, Karma is reflected strongly in a societal caste system. If someone is born in a lower caste, that is their Karma. Any effort to improve their lot is interfering in the possibility they might earn the right, through suffering, to reincarnate to a higher caste next time around. It is literally illegal, therefore, to ease a person's suffering or otherwise do acts of kindness to improve another's lot in life. This is referred to by Hindu law as "altering karma." The penalty is imprisonment or even death.

'to those who will use them for the Kingdom of Heaven, and not for selfish gain.'"

## MYSTERY OF THE KINGDOM #3

### Utilization of the Heavenly Hosts

When asked what the angel looked like, Kemper pauses. "It's so hard to describe the spiritual realm from a physical perspective. But he was glorious; tall and shining. Awesome. Of all the angels I've encountered, he was the most fearsome."

Does Kemper ever see the same angel twice? Yes. He said they seem to have different functions. Some communicate God's messages, while others appear when Kemper is in danger. As an example, Kemper relates the tale of hiking with a group through a mountainous region of Nepal, west of Kathmandu. At a particularly narrow and treacherous portion of the trail, Kemper's foot slipped and the ground gave way beneath him. He began to plummet about 1200 feet. Kemper thought, "Well Lord, I guess this is it." But an angel appeared, caught him and lowered Kemper safely to the ground. "My only injury was a broken finger from grabbing at the rock when I slipped."

When the rest of the group arrived at the bottom of the canyon, thinking they would retrieve Kemper's broken body, they were flabbergasted to find him alive and well. "What took ya so long?" Kemper teased. "I found a short-cut!"[8]

Kemper recognized the same angel during a crucial moment in India. After attending a funeral service, he sat alone not far from the funeral site, eating from a box of chicken he had purchased. Wonderful things had been happening on the trip. Many had professed Christ and more

8 This is Kemper's way when he shares something overwhelming or disturbing. He seeks to lighten the mood, generally with a joke.

suffering children had received aid but Kemper was exhausted. "I was one tired Gringo," he recalls. "I hardly had the energy to bring the food to my mouth."

Looking up from his lunch, he saw two women approaching him. Both had Mongolian-type war axes in their hands. Kemper, who enjoys collecting antiques, took note of the weapons and thought to ask the women if he could buy them. However, as they came closer, the women raised the axes. "They weren't thinkin' about selling. They were gonna use them."

Suddenly the women stopped and stared, wide-eyed, at something behind and above Kemper. They ran away.

When Kemper turned to look, he beheld the same angel who had caught him when falling. "He told me, 'Heavenly servant, look in that direction and be refreshed.' I did what he said and realized, after checking my compass, I was looking east toward Jerusalem. Strength and joy filled me. So beautiful.

"Yes, these incredible things happen, and it's amazing, but it's because I'm doing all this to build the Kingdom of Heaven, not my kingdom, not churchdom. It's not a show. I'm simply the lowest in the Kingdom. But according to Jesus, even the lowest in His Kingdom will do the things He did."

Kemper emphasizes that heavenly encounters occur in need, not on a whim. "It sounds fascinating to talk about seeing angels," Kemper says, "but usually when I see an angel there's no time for fascination because I'm about to die. I see them because I need them."

Kemper says the angels he has encountered always bow subtly in honor of Jesus inside him. "But I don't rejoice that Jesus gives me authority to utilize angelic intervention."

Although angels are glorious, powerful and a vital aspect of Christ's work on earth, true angelic servants of God Almighty will never allow mankind to worship them. To avoid confusion, Kemper usually will not mention angels in the churches where he speaks. "Even though they are co-workers with us to do the work of the Kingdom of Heaven, I like to keep talk about angels to a minimum."

# Chapter Five
# RESISTANCE

**"... bless those who curse you, pray for those who mistreat you."**
**(Luke 6:28, Complete Jewish Bible)**

**"I have learned what it means to suffer for the Kingdom. But I have never learned to feel worthy."**

**~Kemper Crabb**

One day in India, a man ran up to the window of the bus Kemper was riding in, as it paused in traffic. The man had one question: "Do you know Jesus? I'd like to know about him."

Kemper laughs as he remembers his thrilled response. "As a matter of fact, He's a good friend of mine!"

Kemper asked the driver to pull over and he got out to talk to the man who spoke English well, since he sold tea on the streets. As they spoke, more people gathered. Then more. Soon, several interpreters were translating what he said and still the crowd grew. "I climbed up on the hood of the bus, then onto the roof. At one point I thought, 'Lord, how did all these interpreters get here?' Then it hit me; how did *I* get here?"

Kemper kept teaching, explaining the way to God through Christ. Finally, with a crowd that had grown to thousands that blocked the streets, he led them all in prayer for salvation. The entire process took about five hours. Later, an exhausted but elated Kemper went to a nearby house for the night. His friends brought the report that more than 26,000 had prayed for salvation that day.

But resistance came from where he least expected it.

Leaders at his home church did not react to the story with joy. Rather, they were concerned that so many received Christ and yet had no follow-up to help them grow in their newfound faith.

On return trips, Kemper and his team addressed this issue. They built about twenty churches and twenty schools in that area. But Kemper admits he was disappointed in the church leaders' initial reaction.

Sadly, religious opposition was par for the course. On another occasion during his coaching days, Kemper was reprimanded because someone had seen him sitting on the grass close to the college where he taught "with a group of scantily clad young men and women." Kemper laughs at the memory. "I was a coach. We were in gym shorts. What was I supposed to do, teach P.E. in a three-piece suit?"

But the opposition to Kemper's methods went much deeper than attire. When he took groups of people with him to help on his missions, he would have the pastor of the church sign a paper saying the group was an "envoy" from that church. One pastor told Kemper, "I can't sign this. If they go on this trip and see someone healed or raised from the dead, how can I explain that to my people?"[9]

Plus, when ministering in locales where evil is rampant, Kemper needs every heavenly advantage at his disposal, including praying in and speaking in other tongues, plus discerning of spirits, words of knowledge, healing, etc. This practice of the gifts of the Holy Spirit went against the

---

9 Again, Kemper was disappointed in a church leader's reaction but he said this particular pastor has since apologized and has been supportive.

official doctrine of his church. "How could I proceed without the Holy Spirit? It's just not possible. I couldn't even survive one night without relying on the Holy Spirit's gifts and guidance!" Kemper states.

He still speaks to church groups, but he is careful to tailor what he says. "I think one of the reasons for my effectiveness is that I never went to seminary. They teach 'churchdom' not Kingdom." Kemper sees this as an ongoing problem of organized religion. "We had it right up until about 200 AD when we started building these huge cathedrals and church became big business. Church in the New Testament was, 'meet in Phoebe's house.' You meet to worship and you leave to serve."

But according to ministering angels who inform Kemper about what is occurring in the spiritual realm, the greatest problem in the American church is even greater than the rejection of the gifts of the Holy Spirit. "The overriding sin of the West is unforgiveness. In churches, I never understood why there was always an angel facing the west, until it was revealed: it's the forgiveness factor in the western world. That's the great sin of the West, being offended and not forgiving. Jesus came to forgive our sin. We have to forgive others."

MYSTERY OF THE KINGDOM #4:

Covenants[10]: A sacred agreement or pact.

"My family and I made a covenant together to remain unoffended."

In this regard, Kemper refers to the well-known scripture of Matthew 6: 14 & 15 that states clearly, "For if you forgive others for their transgressions,

10 To learn more about the use of covenants in scripture see: Gen. 12: 1-3, Ex. 20: 1-31, Ex. 20: 1-26, 2 Cor. 3: 7-9, 2 Sam. 7: 4-17, 1 Chron. 17: 4-15, Jer. 31: 31-33, Matt. 26: 28 & Gal. 3: 13-20 for starters. For more on covenants go to: https://bible.org/illustration/covenants-scripture

your Heavenly Father will also forgive you. But if you do not forgive others, then your Father will not forgive your transgressions."[11]

Kemper reiterates, "Jesus came to forgive us and we can't forgive someone else? This cuts us off from the Father."

### KEMPER'S CREED

*Father, forgive me in the name of Jesus.*
*I forgive everyone and I love the brethren.*
*I confess that Jesus is Lord; King of Kings,*
*Lord of Lords, Savior, Redeemer, Messiah.*
*Bless, keep, and protect everything You have given me.*
*Send Angels to keep (family, animals, and others).*
*I am seated at the right Hand of the*
*Throne of God.*
*I am covered with the blood of Jesus.*
*Therefore, I take dominion over*
*principalities and powers on earth and*
*in the heavens above.*
*My eyes see, and my ears hear*
*all things physical and spiritual.*
*My body and mind are free from disease*
*and supernaturally protected.*
*So is... (the Spirit of God*
*will give you the names of those*
*to pronounce this Truth upon)*
*Thank You, Father, for the great gift of*
*Salvation You have given me.*

11 See also Matt 5:7, Matt 7:2, Matt. 18:35, Mark 11:25 Col. 3:13 & Eph. 4:32 for a biblical overview of forgiveness.

Kemper's sad summary of the situation: "It's much easier for me to speak to 25,000 in India than to a church here. I'd love to teach people how to do what I do. It's not rocket science. But ya have to put service to the Kingdom of Heaven first, not the kingdom of men."

### Deadly Karma

When he travels to India and Africa, his greatest opposition also comes from organized religion, but that opposition is much deadlier in nature. Usually Kemper runs afoul of government authority in India due to his choice to "alter Karma," an offense punishable by imprisonment and even death.

"Ya see, with this Karma thing," Kemper explains, "say a couple has two children, one healthy and one sickly, and let's say one parent dies and the other is dying. They can give away the healthy child to another home. They're glad to have it. But the sickly child, nobody wants. They will take that child to a back alley and tie them to a post where the child will die alone. You find these little corpses and piles of bones."

Kemper pauses to wipe his eyes. His hands shake as he struggles to control powerful emotions. "We go out during the night and steal those children. We bring them in, get them medical attention, feed them, educate them, and introduce them to Jesus."

According to Hindu law, this represents a criminal altering of Karma. Therefore Kemper has been arrested and marked for murder in India. Wherever he goes, Government agents follow.

But he has discovered unexpected allies.

"The Muslims protect me. They have seen me being kind to their children. That's the way to their hearts." Thus Kemper may have quite an entourage as he ministers in India: government spies and/or soldiers waiting to arrest or harm him, plus self-appointed Muslim guards who have saved his life on more than one occasion.

KEMPER WITH SOME OF "HIS KIDS" IN INDIA

"Once I picked up this little blind child off the street to save him and a van ran off the road at me. It hit the child and killed him then drove away. Some Muslims saw it. They told me, 'The sun will not set on those men again.' They love what I do."

On another occasion, Kemper was invited by a Muslim man to pray for his two sons suffering from Hemophilia. The man said, "I hear some men of your... *persuasion* are able to pray to God for people to be healed." As Kemper spoke with the man, one of the sons, a young man in his twenties, entered the house. Kemper spoke, "The Lord rebuke you, spirit of Hemophilia." The young man fell to the ground. When he came to, the son was healed." Kemper explained the gospel of salvation through Jesus and the young man followed along with Kemper in prayer. "He proclaimed, 'Jesus is my Lord and my God!'"

This same man had a friend who worked in the palace in Kathmandu serving the royal family of King Birendra.[12] When the royal family was

12 King Birendra, also spelled "Bharandra"—reigned from 1972 to 2001. More on King Birendra in Chapter 6. For an overview of his reign and life see: http://en.wikipedia.org/wiki/Birendra_of_Nepal

assassinated, the worker saw the emerald rings on one of the dead royalty. He thought, "The rebels are going to steal these anyway." He removed the rings, cleaned the blood off them and gave them to Kemper. As Kemper is fond of saying, "Ya can't out-give God."

## Imprisoned

Yes, God is generous, but when one purposes to be His servant, suffering is also to be expected.

In his missionary excursions, Kemper has been thrown in prison five times for a total of about one and a half years of incarceration. He says prisons in third-world countries more closely resemble medieval dungeons than modern prisons.

"One time I bought twelve orphan children." Kemper explains that in India's corrupt society, this is often the only way to get the children to safety. "They (his contacts) came to me and said, 'It will cost more. And there are only nine.' Then they opened the basket they carried, and there were the heads of three of the children." Kemper winces as he recalls the horrific sight. "It must have been a federal tip-off." Again, Kemper was arrested.[13]

In India's prisons, there is no heat or sanitation. Prisoners are not fed unless someone brings food from the outside. Kemper survived because his fellow prisoners recognized he was a holy man and did not deserve to be there. The prisoners also noticed, though they were covered with all kinds of vermin, Kemper never had so much as one louse on him. "They knew I was under the protection of my God." Thus the prisoners shared their meager food with him and Kemper, in turn, led most of them to Christ. "They enjoyed singing the old hymns I taught them."

Once, after almost three months incarceration in India, prison guards came to hang Kemper by his hands for three days so he "would not

13 Kemper never found out who betrayed him and killed the children. However, the other nine children did make it to safety. One of them is now a manager over 500 people in an information technology firm and hires as many other orphans as he can to help them get on their feet.

forget." He was strung up so his feet were barely off the floor. "The other prisoners sang, 'On a hill far away, stood an old rugged cross… ' Two of the men puts pieces of rags around the ropes so my wrists would not be cut so severely. This was allowed." When Kemper's shoulders came out of joint, the pain was excruciating. Kemper says one dear man ran forward and crawled beneath his feet to relieve the pain. This was not allowed. "The guards burst in and sliced his throat." Kemper could hear the man's family crying outside when they heard the horrible news. "To hear their wails was terrible suffering for me."

This same man's family cared for Kemper when he was finally released. "They all came to Jesus," Kemper reports.

> "I have learned what it means to suffer for the Kingdom. But I have never learned to feel worthy."

On another occasion, Kemper was incarcerated in the infamous "Black Hole of Calcutta."[14]

However, finding something to laugh about was extremely difficult during his stay in the federal prison. At one point, the prison guards broke his collarbone. "They will make everyone get really quiet so all the prisoners can hear ya scream. It's a way to intimidate." But the guards didn't get what they wanted out of Kemper. "I didn't scream. I passed out."

Why was Kemper imprisoned when his goal is simply to help children? "They accuse me of 'trafficking in human flesh' since I'm willing to pay for the children in order to save them." The real issue is that Kemper

---

14 For a brief history of the "Black Hole of Calcutta": http://www.historytoday.com/richard-cavendish/black-hole-calcutta taken from The Black Hole of Calcutta, an article By Richard Cavendish | Published in History Today Volume: 56 Issue: 6 2006.

is "altering Karma." As stated before, any interruption in the suffering of unfortunates, in the Hindu way of thinking, is cruel because it will prevent that person from reincarnating to a higher caste. This helps to explain the extreme plight of so many in India, whether they are sick, starving, orphaned, leprous or just have the "bad karma" to be poor.

Therefore, when Kemper works in India, caring for children, building hospitals, orphanages, churches and even leprosariums, he is constantly breaking Hindu law. But Kemper is unrepentant and has no plans to honor India's religious hierarchy above the lives of her children.

"This is one of the reasons it's so hard to speak to churches about what I do," Kemper states. "Here I am 'breaking the law' but I'm serving a higher law, Christ's mandate to care for the widows and orphans. In order to do that, I have to... bend a few rules."

But these escapades are always out of obedience to God's mandates, not, as Kemper says, "done on a whim."[15]

15 For an introduction to religion-instigated violence in India see: http://www.telegraph.co.uk/news/worldnews/asia/india/3229253/India-asked-to-investigate-Hindu-massacre-of-Christians.html

# Chapter Six

## THE $2 ALIBI

"No enthusiasm will ever stand the strain that Jesus Christ will put upon His worker, only one thing will, and that is a personal relationship to Himself which has gone through the mill of His spring-cleaning until there is only one purpose left--I am here for God to send me where He will."

-Oswald Chambers

In 2000, a disturbing report reached Kemper while he was in South Calcutta. At one of his orphanages close to an airport in India, armed men had stolen two of the children. Kemper knew time was short if he wanted to save the children from whatever horrors the kidnappers had in store. Plus, he had to send a clear message to those who might attempt similar crimes in the future.

Could he appeal to the local law enforcement?

No. Local authorities were corrupt and Kemper, as a foreigner, did not pull much weight with them.

What could he do?

As is his custom, Kemper sought God's will. His path became clear. It was not politically correct, but clear.

Kemper called upon a friend, a young man who had committed his life to Christ through Kemper's ministry only a couple years before. This young man had a rough background. This young man had a Beretta 9 mm gun.[16]

"We knew where the men were hiding. I went along with him when we... took care of one of them. We got the children back."

Now it was just a matter of details. Kemper and his friend went to the local police. With 50 rupees (about 2 U.S. dollars at the time) he persuaded the officer on duty to enter into the day's books that he and his friend had been arrested for causing a disturbance the night before and had spent the night in jail. "How could we have had anything to do with what happened to those men? We were in jail." Kemper gestures as if pointing to that day's entry. "It says so. Right there."

Again, this is the type of story Kemper will not share in a typical church. He explains that perhaps the best way for Americans to relate to his deeds is from the perspective of a family fighting for their lives in the 1800s during the American expansion westward, when local law was not yet established. Lawlessness reigned. Bullies took advantage. "What I deal with on these trips, with the corrupt government and all, is a completely different world. Children's lives were at stake. I had to act quickly. I had to get the message across, 'Ya don't mess with my kids.'"

Kemper reiterates that his deeds are not self-motivated or self-directed. Neither are they a sweeping generalization of how he conducts his affairs all the time. This was specific direction given in a specific set of circumstances. "This is not for my kingdom; for ego. My authority comes from the One I serve.[17]"

---

16 The Beretta M9 is a 9×19mm Parabellum pistol adopted by the United States Armed Forces in 1985.

17 Mystery of the Kingdom #1

I had to PAY BRIBES to the
tune of Rs 95,000/- and all my
Cases have been WITHDRAWN, and
I have been also issued a New
PassPort, I thank GOD and YOU
for granting me a New Life.
I have been told to be careful
and report anything I find that
is abnormal. Now YOU will get
POLICE PROTECTION when ever you
need the same, when you come
I have to submit a copy of your
PassPort and VISA at the Thakurpukur
Police Station and they will PROTECT
YOU, This is because of the ABDUCTIONS
we are having on Foreigners, this
is for your Safety. DO NOT EVER TEL
ANYONE THAT YOU ARE DOING MISSIONARY
WORK, YOU SAY YOU ARE A TOURIST,
I will take care of the REST.
Do let me know when you are coming
to Thakurpukur, I mean Calcutta.
All send our love and best wishes to
you and hope to see you soon.
I now end,
with Fondest wishes to yo[u]
your Loving Son,

ONE OF KEMPER'S TRUSTED WORKERS WRITES OF THE ONGOING DANGER OF THEIR WORK IN INDIA.

Though his methods are rarely so drastic, Kemper often has to conduct his affairs in spite of the government, finding ways around tricky regulations that would keep him from providing for those in his care.

He has to route money through several channels, through another country—or two—before funds reach his trusted workers and teachers at the churches, schools, orphanages and hospitals. Medicines also follow intricate paths, through other countries, until reaching their intended destination, perhaps even utilizing military transport.

It's not unusual, however, for pathways of provision to appear that can only be explained as divine intervention.

A man in India (name and location withheld to protect the man and those he serves), a Brahmin—meaning he was a member of the highest caste—prayed diligently to learn what he was supposed to do with his life. One day, as he prayed, the man said the sky opened and a voice told him, "Jesus Christ is your Savior and Lord." The man proclaimed, "I have a new birth." God went on to tell him to wait in that place, watching and praying for God's plan for his life to be revealed. For a year and a half the man remained, watchful and praying. When Kemper had a need to protect a group of children he had rescued from the streets, many of whom had been left to die because they were ill or "defective" according to Hindu custom, he drove the children into the hills, praying God would provide a place for them. They stopped at the home of the Brahmin man. "Immediately he knew I and these children were what he had been waiting for," Kemper says.

The man had a large facility there that he, Kemper, and co-workers turned into a school and orphanage.

The story of this particular man and his orphanage/school is one of continuing miracles. Maharajas, who still rule in India's smaller provinces, tend to be quite hostile to the message of Christ.[18]

One Maharaja, violently opposed to Christianity, was backed into a bit of a corner when he needed a school for his own daughters. He happened to live in the area where the Christian Brahmin ran the new school and orphanage. "This Maharaja hates Christians but the teachers in the

18 A Maharaja's position might be compared to a member of the royal family, hereditary and monarch-like.

area give a fifth of their salary to buy the right to go live elsewhere so there are no schools there.[19] But there's *one* school," Kemper says with a triumphant smile, "mine. So his three daughters went to my school and got saved. So much for opposition. It's a bit like Satan guarding Heaven, but it works."

This is one of the reasons Kemper's organization builds a church and school side-by-side, utilizing small, sturdy, useful, simple structures easily accessible to the local populace. "If you get the children, you're gonna get the parents 'cause they're interested in what serves their kids. Plus, this strengthens the community; draws them together."

---

On another occasion, government backing was secured in an even more surprising manner.

Kemper was in Nepal, standing beneath the Ganesh Gate.[20] He sensed the Spirit of God tell him to, "Spoil the Nepalese." This was much like the command given to Moses when he and the children of Israel were leaving Egypt and were told to "Spoil the Egyptians." (Exodus 12:36)

In order to fund his mission work (and per God's instruction), Kemper studied in the early 1990s to become a licensed gemologist. He received his gemology certification in 1994. Kemper proclaims, of all the studying he has done, becoming a gemologist was the most

---

19 This is common practice. It's a bribe of the corrupt government, the results of which hurt the educational prospects of local children.

20 One theory of the origin of Ganesh is that he came to prominence in connection with the four Vinayakas. In Hindu mythology, the Vinayakas were a group of four demons who caused trouble but who were easily appeased. The name Vinayakas is a common name for Ganesh in Hindu worship. Krishan, one of the academics who accepts this view, says of Ganesh, "He is a non-vedic god. His origin is to be traced to the four Vināyakas, evil spirits, of the Mānavagṛhyasūtra (7th–4th century BCE) who cause various types of evil and suffering." Kemper sums up the origin of Ganesh this way, "Two gods had a son, Ganesh, and they decided to behead him. They repented of this action and replaced his head with the head of an elephant. Elephants like bananas so this Ganesh grew up and married a banana tree." With a droll expression Kemper adds, "I don't tend to discuss philosophy with Hindus."

difficult. "You must make a perfect score on *every* exam. *Zero* error." When he travels, he collects precious stones he will later sell in order to fund his work. (More on this in the Chapter titled, *Necessary Miracles.*) At one jeweler in Nepal, he came across a gorgeous, 318 carat topaz. "Absolutely perfect. It's called a 'precious topaz' because it only comes from a mine in northern Burma." Kemper told the jeweler, "I will buy this for 100 American dollars." The jeweler protested but Kemper remained firm, convinced this was what God wanted. He acquired the stone. At another shop he discovered another priceless gem, a huge Siberian Amethyst, "They're so beautiful they'll kill ya," Kemper exclaims. Again, he convinced the jeweler to sell him the 145 carat stone for 100 American dollars.

As he strolled down the street after purchasing the gems, Kemper heard noise behind him. He looked over his shoulder. An angry mob with staves and drawn swords followed him. "They were not trying to renegotiate," Kemper teases.

The experienced adventurer knew exactly what to do under the circumstances.

Run.

Kemper ran until he came to a central colonnade or quadrangle, about ¾ mile long and ¼ mile wide. White horses were moving in formation. About every fifth horse had a wagon behind it. "I jumped up on one of those wagons."

What Kemper did not realize, is that the horses moved in concentric circles as a parade for the Nepalese king and queen. The parade halted. Guards dragged him from the wagon. "You know you'll lose your head for this," a guard assured him.

When brought before the king, Kemper turned on his southern charm. "Oh king, may you live forever."

Kemper was surprised when King Bharandra replied in perfect English, "I'm not Nebuchadnezzar or even Xerxes and you sure as hell aren't Daniel. What are you doing here?"[21]

"Ha! He knew the scriptures. Gotcha!" Kemper seized the divine opportunity. He explained his wish to build churches and orphanages in the area.

"There's no place else on earth where you could have gone to get permission to do this," King Bharandra told him. "Here. Take this to the minister of services."

Kemper not only had official documented permission to build what he wanted in the area—five orphanages and as many churches as necessary—he had a royal decree. Plus, he had the chance to share the most important message of all with the king. "I told him about the King of Kings," Kemper says with a smile.

Later, when Kemper came to town, the king would invite him to dine at the palace.

Kemper will admit he enjoys causing the occasional ruckus, but normally his methods of acquiring gemstones are much simpler and promote good will, not mayhem. On one trip to India, Kemper noticed a lovely sapphire ring on the hand of the man who was driving his bicycle conveyance. He asked the man about the ring. The man was eager to sell the ring since his brother was about to get married and they were seeking money to pay for the ceremony. Kemper could tell the ring was of good quality, no scratches on the beaten metal of the setting, so he asked to buy it. The man quoted a price of 300 rupees and Kemper countered with an offer of 500 rupees. The man was surprised. "Why would you do this?" he asked.

Kemper responded, "I serve Jesus and we like to treat people right."

The man was intrigued. "I've always wanted to know about this Jesus."

---

21 King Bharandra/Birendra had attended Harvard for college, thus his command of the English language.

Right there on the side of the road, Kemper led the man to faith in Christ.

After they prayed, Kemper asked, "What can I do for you?" The man admitted he had been saving up to buy his own auto rickshaw.[22] Kemper ended up loaning the man about 560 dollars for the brand new rickshaw and, with his increased income due to his new work vehicle, the man paid back the money within six months.

So, when Kemper needs to reach places inaccessible to cars, "I just happen to know a guy who owns an auto rickshaw with Servants of the King stickers all over it.

"I also gave him a bumper sticker he put right across the back that says, 'My Dogma Ate My Karma.'" Kemper chuckles. "Aw, that's good!"

---

22 India's answer to the taxi. Think "covered bicycle with a simple lawnmower engine." This link has images: http://www.rickshawchallenge.com/about/the-auto-rickshaw/

# Chapter Seven

## THE LEAST OF THESE

**"For I was hungry and you gave me something to eat, I was thirsty and you gave me something to drink, I was a stranger and you invited me in, [36] I needed clothes and you clothed me, I was sick and you looked after me, I was in prison and you came to visit me."**

**(Matt. 25:35-36 NIV)**

Kemper heard a cry as he walked through a village in India. It was a particular cry of agony he had heard many times before, a sound that always broke his heart. It was the despairing wail of a dying child in extreme pain.

He approached the dwelling. He asked to enter. The mother warned him the children were contagious. She had two who were dying from the Ebola virus. Kemper knew the symptoms. He had seen it too many times. He asked the mother for permission to pray over her children. He went to the first child who lay on a small pallet, burning with fever, eyes glazed with pain. Kemper gently picked up the child and held him close to his chest. He prayed and cried as the child finally closed his eyes and breathed his last. Kemper heard the heavenly trumpets welcoming the child into heaven. He laid the child back on the pallet and moved toward the other sick child, a small girl. "She looked up at me and asked, 'Do you have any love left for me?'"

Kemper chokes on his words and pauses to wipe his nose. "It just breaks your heart."

He picked up the girl's tiny, fevered body, held her close and prayed. Again he felt the angels draw near and heard the heavenly trumpets. "That's what they want when they're dying. People are so afraid of catching their disease, no one will touch them. These children just wanna be loved."

How can Kemper do this for children who are plagued with such a contagious, fatal disease? Unlike most people, his blood is immune to the Ebola virus. "I'm not sure why. I believe it's God's gift so I can love those who are dying."

Over the decades, Kemper has held hundreds of children as they died. He claims it has been the most beautiful and most taxing aspect of his ministry. "Your heart is just broken over and over. I keep waiting to become callous, but… it hasn't happened." Kemper looks up, eyes shining with unshed tears. "But I'll see 'em again in heaven. How glorious that will be?"

**Leprosy**

While Kemper has experienced many miracles and healings in his years of ministry, his duty as a servant is to love and help those no one else will. This is especially needed in India where sickness is viewed as a deserved aspect of karma. Lepers, considered to be the lowest possible caste, receive a large percentage of Kemper's compassion and resources. Sadly, he has never prayed for a leper and seen them miraculously healed. Rather, he says, through the more natural means of proper care and medications, a leper can be cleansed—all for the relatively small price tag of about 145 American dollars. "Those who truly have nothing respond so easily to the message of Christ. There's no pride. They know they're desperate and God is their only possible answer."

Thus Kemper's ministry thrives among the leper colonies. He has even built several hospitals, called leprosariums, solely for the purpose of treating lepers.

"There is one man, a leper in Darjeeling, who I led to Christ several years ago. He dedicated his life to spreading the message of Jesus in the leper colony even though I invited him to go to the hospital. 'No,' he said. 'My place is here.' He wanted to spend every moment he had left spreading God's love to the people in that colony."

Kemper had the great honor of watching this man's transition into glory. "He had a little broken bracelet with a white stone. He gave it to me and said, 'It's all I have. I give it to you because you gave me Jesus.' Then he went and sat with his back to a tree. His face was so disfigured from leprosy, nose missing and such, but at the last moment I got a glimpse of his transformation (into his heavenly body). His face was whole. He smiled. Such peace. Then I heard the trumpets."

**Malaria**

Malaria is one of the most virulent killers in India and Africa. In fact, malaria was one of the major contributing factors in the death of Mother Teresa.[23]

A huge blessing in Kemper's life is that he has discovered a very inexpensive cure for the mosquito-borne disease. Here's the real kicker: his cure costs about half a penny per person. It's a simple, common compound, but pharmaceutical companies would be against the discovery because this cure could not receive a patent. It's too common. What to do?

Once more, Kemper can accomplish much more by keeping a low profile. Plus, as a former coach, Kemper understands the natural tendency for folks to be motivated, according to King Solomon's statement in Ecclesiastes 4:4, regarding "rivalry." Simply put, competition can be a

23 Mother Teresa suffered from heart problems and, toward the end of her life in 1997, her heart was further weakened by complications due to Malaria.

great motivator.[24] He went to the leaders of the Kiwanis Club. He told them, "The Rotary Club wiped out Polio. What have you done?"

Therefore, his malaria hospital on an island in Africa has an inscription over the door—The Kiwanis Club insignia. Once again, Kemper's aim is not personal glory, it's all for the Kingdom of Heaven. To accomplish this aim, he has to remain on his guard and one step ahead of bureaucratic red tape. Kemper flashes a triumphant smile. "The pharmaceutical companies could come after one person, but how do they go after a whole organization with thousands of chapters across the United States?"

24 Ecc. 4:4 "I have seen that every labor and every skill which is done is the result of rivalry between a man and his neighbor. This too is vanity and striving after wind." NASB

# Chapter Eight
## MOTHER T.

**"Not all of us can do great things, but we can all do small things with great love."**

**Mother Teresa**

Kemper followed the young man through India's poverty-stricken back alleys. Although the young man, Nelson,[25] was friendly, sincere, and one of Kemper's main contacts in Calcutta, Kemper was on his guard. Nelson worked for the Mennonites and said he had known Mother Teresa since he had been cared for by the saintly nun as a young orphan and had helped her tend to lepers and the severely impoverished.

But Kemper was not popular with the Indian government and there had been several attempts on his life, therefore he was wary of Nelson's motives. Plus, Kemper knew it was very difficult to gain access to Mother Teresa, since she tended to shun unwanted attention, especially on her home turf. "Ya had more chance of an audience with the Pope than to meet her," Kemper states. Therefore when Nelson asked Kemper, "Want

25 Name changed

to meet Mother T?" Kemper had responded with a skeptical, "Yeah, right."

But the young man stopped in front of a two-story structure and called up toward a window, "Mother T! Mother T! Come out. There is someone I want you to meet."

A tiny woman clad in the well-known white garb with blue sash came to the window. The young man had been telling the truth. He really *was* friends with Mother Teresa.

Kemper introduced himself and gave her his card that identified him as an Episcopal priest. "Where are you going, Episcopal servant?" Mother T. asked.

"I'm going up into the mountains to build churches and schools," Kemper informed.

Mother Teresa's reply surprised him. "Then come around to the back. I'll go with you. They're driving me crazy here!"

KEMPER (R) WALKS WITH MOTHER TERESA AND ANOTHER PASTOR

Kemper pauses to chuckle. "She was so funny. Most people don't know that."

So the famous, tiny nun who had captured the world through her humanitarian deeds among India's outcasts befriended the missionary from Texas. Their ministry to unfortunates was not the only thing they had in common. Mother T. and Kemper also shared a love for poetry.

"We used to make people so mad," Kemper recalls. "We had this sort of game we would play where one would start a poem and the other would finish it. Folks'd say, 'Oh no. There they go again!'"[26]

Kemper was shocked a couple years later to learn Mother Teresa had nominated him for a Nobel Peace Prize.[27] Kemper likes to joke that, in regards to the Nobel, he's a three-time loser. Though he was never awarded the prize, he says his nominations performed a very important function. "My association with Mother Teresa gave me some notoriety so I was no longer thrown in prison in India. I think they were very conscious of looking bad as far as international relations."

Kemper's recollections of Mother Teresa are of a selfless servant of God who always tried to turn the spotlight toward others. "Although," Kemper admits, "if there was a chance to stir up funds for the lepers, orphans and others she cared for, she could be quite canny. She never passed up an opportunity for that."

At one point, Kemper took a simple, two-inch, maple wood cross as a gift to Mother Teresa. "From then on, she kept that little cross in her pocket."

When Kemper learned of Mother Teresa's passing, he grieved the death of his friend and fellow servant. "But she's got to be so happy surrounded by all the children she helped through the years."

---

26 When asked why poetry was so special to him, Kemper explained that when he was in prison, he had a habit of poring over whatever he had committed to memory. He said this kept him from losing his mind. He would repeat memorized scripture and poetry. It also helps that Kemper, the boy doctors said would have brain damage, has a photographic memory.

27 Kemper has been nominated for the Nobel three times; once by Mother Teresa, once by King Bharandra & once by "The Crown of Great Britain."

What of the cross Kemper had given to her? "The Sisters of Charity returned it to me. Mother T. had told them, 'Give this back to the Episcopal Servant.'"

Of all the precious items in his care, the simple, small cross is the most prized. "I've had people say they got a shock of power when they touched it. I guess if anyone could have infused something with God's love just by keeping it with her, it would have been Mother T."

Kemper adds, "I guess I could sell it to the Catholic Church and build another hospital with the money. She'd probably like that."

Update: On one of Kemper's recent airline flights, (Spring of 2014) a businessman from Albania sought him out. The man heard there was a fellow passenger who had worked with Mother Teresa. He had also heard of the cross that was in Kemper's possession. The man found Kemper and sat next to him on the airplane in order to make a request. He had the desire to build a shrine at Mother Teresa's birthplace in Albania. He asked to purchase the cross to serve as the central icon of the shrine.

With that money, Kemper plans to build another hospital.

# Former Huntsville resident returns as a Nobel Peace Prize nominee

**By PAUL STURROCK**
The Huntsville Item

A former Huntsville resident who toils among the lowest of the low is returning to describe the good works that made him a nominee for the Nobel Peace Prize.

Kemper Crabb, a Huntsville High School and Sam Houston State University graduate, has devoted himself to others since 1984 when he began organizing

said Norman Ward, a member of th Huntsville Rotary Club that will he Crabb speak Wednesday.

"He's a very down-to-earth, look yo straight in the eye kind of guy. There nothing phony about him."

Ward said probably 100 percent donations for Crabb's undertakings g strictly toward sturdy, utilitarian faciliti for the unfortunate.

"He can do it very economically

News of Kempers Nobel nomination reached Texas newspapers

# Chapter Nine
## RECKLESS ABANDON

**"Paul (The Apostle) was not conscious of himself. He was recklessly abandoned, totally surrendered, and separated by God for one purpose— to proclaim the gospel of God."**

**-Oswald Chambers**

**"Though He slay me, yet will I trust him."**

**(Job 13:15 NKJV)**

It was the 1970s. Kemper was a coach at San Antonio College. Among his athletes and weight-training students he noticed a trend. There were certain times when his students could lift more weight; when the weights seemed actually lighter. What was causing this phenomenon?

Kemper recalled the scripture, "Call unto me and I will answer thee and show thee great and mighty things which thou knowest not." *(Jer. 33:3 KJV)* He prayed and asked God to show him the key.

That night, Kemper had a dream about the moon. When he woke, he began researching lunar phases. He incorporated this lunar data into the weight-training schedule. "Wonderful thing was I had all these guinea pigs, er, *students* to test my theories on," Kemper teases.

What Kemper discovered was that two to four days before a new lunar phase, there was more resistance. There would be *less* resistance, however, the day on or the first day after a new lunar phase.

The revised schedule had an immediate positive effect. However, Kemper felt there was another piece of the puzzle necessary for optimal results. Once more he prayed about the issue.

"I had another dream where I could see angels walking upon the waves of the ocean. I knew I needed to learn about the *tides*."

More research resulted in more tweaking of the weight schedule to account for moon phases plus tidal patterns. "Then voila!" says Kemper. "We had it!"

Thus his assigned workouts for students were a bit eclectic. "I could say, 'You, come in at two a.m. on this day' and so forth." In this way, Kemper was able to test and adjust his theories about how the tides and lunar phases affect strength. "Basically, when the moon is full, it has an effect on gravity *and* on the person. The weights feel lighter. It moves the waves in the ocean. This has an effect on us too."

Not all the students who incorporated this new regimen were athletes. "I was using this on just regular students too and everyone began to lift much more. Our goal was to improve weight-lifting ability by 300 percent."

**(A note from one of Coach Crabb's former weight training students)**

*COACH*

*I'm a girl who endured secondary education in the 60s. That was when P.E. didn't mean physical education. It meant "Did you wash your whites over the weekend?' "Physical" meant up to but not including sweat. "Education" meant memorizing a square dance. P. E. teachers were the ladies who handed you the appropriate ball, pointed toward the appropriate area of the playground, and told you the appropriate time to come back for the next real class.*

*Twenty years later: my first encounter with a Coach.*

*He's going to teach me weight training. His first speech is the context for the relationship he will have with us. I sense something authentic is happening. He says the course will demand real work and real sweat.*

*He says, "If that's not your intention, drop this course now and get some of your money back."*

*He says, "Have your physical examination form in my hand before 10 a.m. Thursday or don't let me see you here. "*

*He says, "Here's where I stand in life. I'm a Christian, and in here 'Thou shalt be all you can be.' Now take two!"*

*I thought he meant aspirin because that idea was building already. The boys knew he meant two miles. Give me a break. Not a chance. Two miles in the noon heat?*

*The young man next to me in the alphabetical roll call wanted to give his great excuse for not having his physical form at the next class. Coach looked past him with a crisp "out." He meant what he said.*

*How can life be so marvelously well-designed that this coach is named "Crabb?" "Commander Crabb" is more like it.*

*The two-mile run is through San Pedro Park. Pounding, breathing, pounding, breathing. Coach isn't back in the teachers' lounge. You come upon him suddenly after a turn. He's standing erect, attentive to our effort, sometimes barely nodding his approval as we pass. He's been teaching for twenty-nine years. Why does he have such intensity? I'm probably his 10,000th student. Why is it like each of us is his first?*

*The smallest girl he calls "Conan." The cutest, "Smurfette." The fattest boy he wants to "see less of you next week… say about ten pounds less of you."*

*He barked his disapproval when our attention wavered. The boys had had a coach before and knew to do better—no problem. The girls learned men can yell and it doesn't mean we have to cry. It means he yelled. This secret, men have learned from coaches. My daughters will have a coach.*

*Every day after the panting weight lifting, I think he might let up on the run. It's August. It's so hot. But he never cheats us.*

*"Take two!"*

*By Martha White,*
*Former Servants of the King Board Member & Historian*
*Former Student of "Coach Crabb"*

COACH CRABB

When Kemper's students began to win weight-lifting competitions and some even advanced to Olympic status, word got around. *Way* around. In fact, word reached China.

Dr. Wang, chairman of China's Olympic Committee, sent China's top weightlifter, Eu Gen Son, for training. Dr. Wang then came for his own visit. When Kemper asked Dr. Wang where he was on his own spiritual journey, Dr. Wang pointed to his own heart and responded, "Jesus." He ended up inviting Kemper to speak at the Asian games about his groundbreaking regimen. Kemper also spoke at all the major universities in China in 1989. Never one to overlook an opportunity to spread the good news of Christ, Kemper added another aspect to his speeches. "They told me I could talk about whatever I wanted, so I also told them about The Kingdom of Heaven."

This was Socialist China at a time when the Chinese government was persecuting Christians. Yet this football coach with a unique approach to weight training was allowed to speak all over China about salvation through Jesus and the Kingdom of Heaven? The improbability of this situation was not lost on Kemper. "God works in mysterious ways His wonders to perform."[28]

Kemper too was always in excellent health and participated in his own weight-training schedule. He reports that when he was 70 he could still bench press six reps of 300 pounds.

But health was another blessing Kemper had to risk in order to continue serving Christ. Through his years of service he has been beaten, imprisoned, tortured and even stoned. He felt the wear and tear, but he believed his time on earth would be short. "For instance, I never gave much thought to having to renew my passport. I truly thought I wouldn't live long enough to worry about it."

---

28 "God moves in a mysterious way His wonders to perform" are the first two lines of a Hymn written by William Cowper (1731-1800). This was reportedly the last hymn Cowper wrote. There is a powerful (though unsubstantiated) story about Cowper attached to the writing of this hymn. Go to: http://www.sweetsongministries.com/id98.html.

Then on a trip to Africa in October of 2005, Kemper received a near-fatal spider bite. Usually this particular spider's venom—most likely what is known as a "banana spider," fourteen times more venomous than the black widow—kills within a few days. It was touch-and-go for Kemper. He lived, but lime disease settled into his joints and the toxin threatened his heart. Finally, this robust former football star and weight-training coach felt his age. "I think, if I hadn't gone through prison, torture, and such, I couldn't have stood that pain."

By God's Grace
The Order
Servants of the King
John 12:26

Redemption of Souls
Alleviation of Suffering

January 30, 2006

Dearest Friends,

Help! I am in trouble. I desperately need your intercessory prayers. My body has been stricken with a strange malady. Within 4 to 7 days all of the joints, from my toes to my fingers, have become severely painful. It is as though the entire body has become arthritic. If you have ever had the flu, you know the feeling.

My dad used to tell me, "It's not the year, it's the miles that take a toll on you." I don't know if it is the hundreds of suffering children I have picked up, the great number of lepers I have treated, or the hundreds of thousands of people I have walked among proclaiming the Kingdom of God over the past 20 plus years. While it is true that East Africa is not even a fraction as difficult as Asia, it is still a burden.

In all of the orphanages, hospitals, and places of sanctuary I have built for children I always provide a pet. A child will learn to treat other children and people with the same love and kindness they treat a sweet little pet. I usually get a mongoose, kitten or puppy. Sometimes the pet will die. The children ask "Grandfather, why did it die?" I usually tell them, "It was his time to go."

Most of the children are terminal by the time I get them. They almost always remember what I told them about the pet's demise. Knowing their time is near at hand, they will come to me and say, "Grandfather, it's my time to go, will you hold me?" As I hold them, and their little soul goes out into eternity, there is a felt presence of Holiness as the Angels of God come for them. After holding 3 or 4 hundred of them my heart is broken. Even my very soul is torn.

Perhaps it is "My time to go."

Loving you and the Kingdom of God,

Kemper

Kemper B. Crabb
P.O. Box 781903 San Antonio, TX 78278

A LETTER KEMPER SENT OUT TO SERVANTS OF THE KING MEMBERS AFTER THE NEAR-FATAL SPIDER BITE.

This experience also prompted Kemper to give thought to who would carry on his ministry when he was no longer able. While there are key individuals who oversee aspects of his various businesses—coffee plantations, tree plantations, land ventures, gemology, and even a recording studio—and others run the various orphanages, schools and churches, finding someone to undertake the many roles Kemper fills is a tall order. "It's hard to convince folks to put their lives on the line for no salary," Kemper quips. "Again, what I do is not rocket science. Ya just do the things Jesus did. And you do it with *intensity.*"

It's also difficult to find someone willing to work without notoriety. "Most churches and organizations know what to do with ya if you have a big name and a big following. They don't quite know what to do with me. I'm not even coming with my hat in my hand asking for money. It's like I'm speaking a totally different language."

However, along with his three Nobel Prize nominations, Kemper has had his share of opportunities for prestige. In fact, after his round of talks in China, he had offers from Ivy League universities to take a position as a fulltime professor. "I went to visit. It was beautiful. I thought, 'I could *be* somebody.' 'Cause I realize in the eyes of the world I'm a nothin." Kemper shrugs, "I gotta be honest. It was tempting."

"What I do is not rocket science. Ya just do the things Jesus did.
And you do it with intensity."

He turned down the offer in order to continue pouring his efforts into those who cannot give back—at least not with prestige and a flourishing bank account.

But when Kemper speaks of the children who line the streets of African villages shouting "Simba! Simba!" to hail his arrival, or the joy of leading a large crowd to accept Christ, or the gratitude on a leper's face when he receives medical attention, or the contented smile of a child who snuggles into his arms with one last breath before crossing into Heaven, there is not even a hint of regret.

Kemper says the glories of serving The Kingdom and the thrill of knowing God's approval far outweigh the troubles and dangers. "I'm laying up treasures in Heaven."

**A Glorious Airport Encounter**

The constant heartbreak and physical duress are draining. Kemper admits there are moments when even he leans toward despair. Luckily, God finds ways to encourage.

On a trip back home in Spring of 2014, Kemper was waiting in an Indian Airport. He says the great numbers of people in Calcutta overwhelmed him and in his exhausted frame-of-mind, he asked, "God, how can I possibly make a difference here?"

The gate where Kemper awaited his flight had no chairs available for him. A concerned Muslim woman offered to give him her seat. Kemper said, "No thank you. The Lord bless you," and made a swift sign of the cross over her head. His body ached with fatigue so Kemper moved to another area where he found a place to sit down.

Soon the woman sought him out to ask, "What did that sign mean that you made with your hand?" Kemper told her he was a servant of Christ and his hand gesture was the sign of the cross. She asked to hear more. Kemper was more than willing to oblige. Right there in a crowded airport, he led the woman to salvation. After praying, the excited woman left him only to return soon with about thirty-three other women, most of whom wore the traditional Muslim veil over their faces. He also shared the message of salvation through Jesus with them. Excitement fills his voice as Kemper reports their enthusiastic reaction to the gospel. "Soon they were all praising God and pulling away the coverings over their faces as they proclaimed, 'Jesus is my Savior and Lord!'"

Even with Kemper's many years of ministry, the experience of leading people to Christ and observing their transformation and joy as they discover freedom from the inside-out never grows old for him. "Isn't that beautiful!" he exclaims. "I was still tired but, aw, it's so worth it!"

Kemper continues to plan new ventures; inaugurating churches, building hospitals, churches, schools, orphanages and seminaries. He is even establishing work in new countries although he admits his recovery from trips these days takes a bit longer. "I'm tired *from* the work I do, not tired *of*."

Kemper looks forward to the moment when the Heavenly trumpets he has heard for so many others announce *his* time to pass into eternity.

"My name is written in the Lamb's Book of Life. *That's* my reason to rejoice."

KEMPER AT THE PROPOSED SITE OF ANOTHER UGANDAN VILLAGE CHURCH

## Help Wanted: International Missionary/Apostle

Must:

*Pay for own on-the-job training
*Excel at spiritual warfare
*Possess excellent business experience
*Possess excellent negotiating skills
*Overflow with love for the unlovable
*Exhibit unflagging persistence
*Find a way to laugh when broken-hearted
*Endure lengthy separations from home & family
*Seek no personal monetary reward

Possible Dangers:

*Imprisonment
*Assassination Attempts
*Torture
*Poisonous insects
*Deadly, wild animals
*Demonic attacks
*Frequent Hunger
*Uncomfortable accommodations
*Exposure to fatal illnesses
*Frequently misunderstood, slandered and/or cursed

Any takers?

# Chapter Ten
## SUPERNATURAL

**"For our struggle is not against flesh and blood, but against the rulers, against the authorities, against the powers of this dark world and against the spiritual forces of evil in the heavenly realms."**

**(Eph. 6:12 NIV)**

The worship of evil, better known as juju or voo-doo, has a powerful grip on the third world cultures where Kemper ministers. They do not need to be convinced of the spiritual realm. What they seek is to be set free from the fear of what they know is real.

"They latch onto witchcraft and such because they feel powerless. They don't like it but it's the only way they know to get help," Kemper explains.

If left unchecked, this involvement in evil can result in phenomena seemingly more suited to horror movies.

**Stranger Than Fiction**

Kemper and a man who often accompanied him on his ventures in Africa were on a trip from Nepal to West Bengal, about to cross through a military checkpoint on their trip. There was a problem. It was past the curfew for civilians to be out and about, plus they were attempting to enter a restricted zone. As they approached the guard shack, their headlights piercing the darkness, Kemper and his driver muttered nervous prayers. "All of a sudden we're surrounded by soldiers and have AK 47s aimed at us. One of the soldiers asks, 'What is your place of origin?'" Kemper had a response that tends to intrigue the Indian soldiers. "I told him I was from Texas. If they don't know that's a part of the United States, they don't want to appear ignorant."

The soldier's face lit up, "Ah! The Alamo!" The soldier loved the movie starring John Wayne and was thrilled to meet someone from that legendary locale.

After a short conversation about Davy Crockett, Kemper and his friend were allowed to pass. The soldier even told them about a route that would avoid further checkpoints.

Later on, they were driving a few miles south of Calcutta when their headlights shone on a man who stared at them from the bushes and trees that lined the deserted road. "He was in the process of changing, his face elongating and fangs appearing." What Kemper describes next sounds like the result of special effects make-up and Hollywood trick photography. He and his companion saw the man quickly transform into a classic werewolf form. "I've seen several encounters of people changing like that and it's considered 'fake' or whatever. But it's not."

Kemper's friend was not responding well to the encounter. "He tends to have this... malady; a certain bladder issue when he is suddenly scared. But I was grabbing for my camera to get a picture. So here we are, he's wet his britches, I'm grabbin' for my camera and we're laughin' as this guy just goes loping off."

**A Deadly Interruption**

On another occasion, Kemper was in the middle of sharing the gospel in one of his small churches in Africa when a man came in shouting obscenities. Kemper, prompted by God's directive, took control of the situation. He said, "The Lord rebuke you!"

Working in hostile spiritual territory often brings the need for spiritual warfare. Kemper was used to rebuking those bent on opposing what God told him to do. However, on this occasion, the effect was stunning.

As soon as the words were off Kemper's tongue, the angry man fell down dead.

The people who witnessed this altercation ran from the church in fright. "But I knew they'd be back so we took the body outside, buried him, and went on with the service. When the people returned, they brought more people with them. We ended up having 4020 saved."

### A Supernatural Prison Break

On an outreach to China, Kemper was thrown into prison. Despite his inability to speak Russian and his marked Texas drawl, he was accused of being a Soviet spy due to the brand of binoculars he carried. "This place was inside a mountain. Inescapable. It's the kind of prison people just don't leave. At least not alive."

After several weeks of handcuffs and near-starvation, Kemper was weak and sickly. His captors brought him out for more questioning. As Kemper stood, shackled and, for the moment, ignored by the jailers who had turned away to converse, he lifted a prayer to God. "Lord, if you don't do somethin', I'm gonna die in here."

> "I found myself outside those walls. I don't even remember passing through them. I was just there."

Kemper saw a set of keys on the desk. He reached for them. No one noticed. He unlocked his chains. Still, miraculously, no one looked his way. "There's nothing as encouraging as success, so I reached into the drawer of the desk where I had seen them put my personal belongings."

As soon as his passport and other items were in his hands, another miracle occurred.

"I found myself outside those walls. I don't even remember passing through them. I was just there."

But there was no time or energy for celebration. "I was in a bad way—starving, beat-up. I was still gonna die if I didn't get help quick."

Kemper stumbled down the mountain to a nearby road where he was able to catch a ride to Shrinagar. He recovered a bit there then started walking toward New Delhi hoping to catch a bus. Soon a group of merchants from the Kyber pass picked him up and took him down through New Delhi. They were kind, placing him atop one of the camels—a dromedary—the breed with the big hump. Every jolt on that road shot pain through Kemper, who still had a couple broken bones, so they switched him to a double-humped camel, known for having a smoother gait.

"They were so, so sweet to me," Kemper recalls. They could all see he was touched by their kindness. Kemper got to tell them about the Kingdom of Heaven and many of the merchants professed faith in Christ. Soon, the merchants brought Kemper to the American consulate building. He was safe. He would get to go home.

**Resurrections**

In 1990, Kemper was traveling toward Lucknow in northern India. He and those with him, including four of their orphan children and workers from one of Kemper's schools, found themselves in the midst of a Pooja. A Pooja is a Hindu religious festival. As their van threaded its way through the huge crowd, an elderly woman stepped out from the side of the road and their van hit her. "She was immediately killed," says Kemper. "She was mangled badly."

A mob from the Pooja came toward the van, drawing their swords, ready to execute vengeance on those responsible for killing one of their own. Besides, according to Hindu belief, this would insure a higher reincarnation for them.

One of Kemper's companions was ready to accept the inevitable. "We must put this in the hands of God."

Kemper replied, "God has put this in *my* hands." He got out of the van and went to the woman who was obviously dead. "Her bones were broken and showing. Her head was oozing cranial fluid."

Once more, God gave Kemper the words to say. "God rebuke you, death, in Jesus' name. Live!"

Everyone in the area fell. The only one standing was Kemper who, according to those with him, was glowing. The woman sat up, the blood gone, her bones straight. She dusted herself off, as if she had simply fallen in the dirt, and acted slightly confused as to how she got there.

Kemper, at a bit of a loss as to what to do, told those nearby to give her something to eat. "After all, that's what Jesus always said when someone came back from the dead." Then, taking advantage of the crowd's amazement, Kemper and his companions prepared to drive away.

But God was not finished with this situation and had further direction for Kemper. "The Spirit said to me, 'Don't leave these people with impunity.[29] They tried to destroy My servant. Speak an imprecation.'[30] So I turned in my seat and spoke, 'God, carry out Your plan on these people according to their deeds.'"

Kemper and his crew drove on to a small town where they found a resting place for the night. His companions protested that it was impossible

29 impunity: exemption or freedom from punishment, harm, or loss.

30 imprecation: a curse. Many of the Psalms are called "imprecatory Psalms" since David was asking God to reward his enemies according to their evil deeds.

for them to stay there because it was only for the upper class, the Top Brahmans, and was very exclusive and expensive. But Kemper, exhausted from sleeping on porches in the frigid cold and traveling without proper meals, insisted. "We got three rooms, and ate three good meals unlike anything they had ever had. The total cost of the rooms and meals was under $28. They thought I was rich."

The next morning, there was talk of a horrible earthquake in the northwest that had opened the ground and swallowed 3000 people.[31]

Kemper and his companions pondered the news. "It was then that what had happened struck them. One of them exclaimed, 'That woman was dead and you called her back to life!'" They also remembered the words of imprecation Kemper had uttered and the fact this earthquake occurred where the mob had wanted to kill them.

But this particular missionary excursion had more astounding events in store for Kemper and his companions.

Later that morning, they drove through Lucknow, India, the capital of Utar Pradesh, a city of approximately seven million. Lucknow was reported at the time to only have about five Christian families.

In the horrible traffic, typical for a large Indian city, they were stopped by a police officer. The little Mitsubishi they drove was packed with Kemper, three other adults and four orphans they had saved off the streets. The police officer asked their driver for his license then proceeded to take it away. Another man in the car said, "Don't worry. I still have my license." The police officer overheard this statement and confiscated the second license as well.

31 Taken from: http://earthquake.usgs.gov/earthquakes/world/world_deaths.php) "In October of 1990, two events occurred about 1.6 seconds apart. At least 2,000 people killed, more than 1,800 injured and 18,000 buildings destroyed in the Chamoli-Uttarkashi area. Some damage occurred at Chandigarh and New Delhi. Felt in northern India, western Nepal and northeastern Pakistan. Landslides occurred in the epicentral area. A 30-meter deep crack was noted in the Uttarkashi area."

Kemper got out of the car to see what was causing the delay. There was a gigantic intersection of six or seven roads. Kemper wove his way up to the center where there was a tremendous commotion. At the center of the crowd was a little girl, dead and covered with flies, while people wailed and carried on their mourning practices, dancing and cutting themselves.

Kemper notes that crowds in India are unimaginably huge, like 50 to 100 thousand strong. He walked up to the girl and said, "God rebuke you, death, in the name of Jesus." The girl immediately revived, and the crowd was amazed.

A man ran up to Kemper and asked, "By what god's power have you done this miracle?"

Kemper replied, "I thought you'd never ask." He launched into the story that the first martyr, Stephen, told the crowd who were about to stone him (Acts, Ch. 7). Kemper spoke of the Israelites in Egypt and eventually of the salvation story of Jesus. God provided translators. "I did hope," Kemper quips, "that my story would have a better ending than Stephen's did." In this way, the story Kemper told, plus the way to be saved by calling on the name of Jesus, passed throughout the huge throng of people.

The next morning, Kemper was woken before sunrise by sounds of excitement and shouting. Apparently, the good news Kemper had told had spread throughout the town. The men with him said that 112,000 people had professed faith in Christ!

Also though, the messengers reported that Lucknow authorities were angry that Kemper had caused a disturbance in the town. Kemper would have to flee. He had been intending to go to Islamabad, but he was told men were already in Islamabad ready to capture and imprison him. Instead, he went down to Calcutta. This was Kemper's first of many visits to that notorious city.

When Kemper got home from India, he discovered news of the earthquake in Northern India had been reported in Texas. One of their friends at church, knowing Kemper was in north India, had asked Kemper's wife Tommye if she knew about the earthquake. Tommye had replied, "No, but he probably caused it!"

Kemper laughs. "She knows me well. She also knows our God well and His protection over His servants who give up who they are, take up His cross and follow Him into the world."

February

The San Antonio Christian Beacon

*"Let your light so shine before men that they may see your good deeds and praise your Father in heaven"*
*Matthew 5:16*

Volume 11, Issue Number Two — *San Antonio's monthly newspaper serving the Christian community* — February 2002

## Local Missionary Brings 883,000 to Christ

*By Barbara Marques*

A talk with Kensington Cromwell about his missionary work is more than just a casual conversation, it's a lesson in scripture, world history, geography, philosophy and sociology.

Retired from a 25-year career as a professor, coach and athletic director of San Antonio Community College, Cromwell, for the past 15 years, has followed Someone Else's game plan. He is called to do the work of the Lord. As a missionary in northern India and central Africa, Cromwell has endured imprisonment in Calcutta, walked among wild tigers and cobras and been exposed to a myriad of diseases, including leprosy, malaria, ebola, and AIDS. But, he claims, the angels have protected him and he has never been seriously injured or ill.

As a part of his work through his non-profit organization, Servants of the King, Cromwell is credited with the building of 19 orphanages, 3 large leprosy hospitals and hundreds of churches in northern India, a place where few missionaries will go because of its treacherous wildlife and dangerous social conditions.

He has also built thousands of churches and one large AIDS hospital in Uganda, Africa. In late January, Cromwell left on yet another mission trip into northern India to inaugurate churches and continue the building process.

Though the work is dangerous, it has its rewards – like the satisfaction of knowing that he has literally rescued from death, hundreds of starving and diseased children – or the fact that Servants of the King has seen roughly 883,000 converts come to Jesus from Hinduism or Islam. That number may seem staggering, except when you consider the fact that, according to Cromwell, the city of Calcutta alone has a population of 35 million (compare that to the approximately 22 million that live in the entire State of Texas).

Cromwell is a spirited man, with a lively sense of humor and many adventurous tales to share. In fact, his missionary tales are published as episodes and distributed by his organization, Servants of the King. However, Cromwell remains well-grounded in the Word. Every story he shares incorporates scripture and gives God the honor and glory for all of the progress in India and Africa.

Cromwell has jokingly dubbed himself a "three-time loser" – referring to the fact that he has been nominated for the Nobel Prize on three separate occasions. His nominations came from such noteable folks as Mother Teresa, Prime Minister Margaret Thatcher and the King of

See Missionary Page 3

**Walking with Legends on the Same Path**
*San Antonio Missionary Kensington Cromwell walks with Mother Teresa and others on their missionary team. Cromwell worked with Mother Teresa building churches in the Sunderbahn, just south of Calcutta.*
Courtesy Photo

**Caring for the Children**
*Travelling where no missionary has in 185 years, Cromwell cares for the children who have no one else.*

**Caring for the Suffering**
*Cromwell has built three large leprosy hospitals, like the one pictured above, in India. It is estimated that 1.5 million children*

## Creator of Local Children's Show is The Cat's Meow

*By Kathy Roberts*

I see her on television and hear her music played over and over again on the stereo in our family room. Very rhythmic, lots of movement. I look up to see a carrot-top woman in a tye-died shirt doing some sort of exercise on the screen surrounded by enthusiastic children and adults. My children are moving to the beat. They are smiling. They twirl, they tumble, they laugh. "Great stuff," I think to myself and stop to watch the woman who has mesmerized my little ones. As I watch, I also tune into the words. Although I've heard the songs a hundred times, they sound familiar in a different way. "Therefore I tell you, do not worry, seek first the Kingdom and all will be right." Now I know. It's a verse from The Book. Wow! – On television. I like it.

Her name is Lee Campbell-Towell – "Miss Lee" as she is affectionately referred to – and she is the inspiration and the energy behind the wildly popular children's show Cat Paws, which airs on KLRN-PBS TV, satellite television nationwide, and StarNet which airs in public schools. Quite similar her music, they love the rhythm, and they love the funky movements that make her music come alive. What children may not know, but parents should, is that her music has a message. A powerful message for Believers and non-believers alike. "If you're a Christian, you know what the song – the scripture – is saying. If you're not a Christian, you are getting the positive message anyway. It's exciting to share His message." There was a lot I was surprised to learn about this petite firecracker of a woman. Dynamic and energized with children, she is relaxed and informal in her "off time." Her recollections of the past and vision for the future spill forth effortlessly with warmth and a distinct sense of direction.

It all started in 1991 when her first book of songs was published. Although she has written music throughout her life, it wasn't until she had a child that she started writing music for children. Before long she

children's songs. As an elementary school teacher, she saw the value of combining music and movement. According to Towell, "it's not dancing – it's a combination of movement and music that teaches motor skill development." In addition to motor skill development, she focuses on the positive sound and the positive messages for kids. "The more good things you put in a child, the more good things will come out of that child."

**The Inspiration for Cat Paws**
*"Miss Lee" is the friendly, smiling face recognized by children throughout San Antonio and South Texas*

LOCAL NEWSPAPERS IN TEXAS BEGAN TO TAKE NOTICE OF KEMPER'S EXPLOITS

Though Kemper has never returned to Lucknow, a fellow Servants of the King worker, Lanny Green, traveled to Lucknow, India in 2010 for a meeting of all Christian pastors in the area. Green reported that Lucknow is known now as "a hotbed of Christianity" since its populace contains, for India, a very high percentage of those who profess faith in Jesus.

# Chapter Eleven

## FIRST THINGS FIRST—SPIRITUAL WARFARE

**Everything that *is* has been created. In order for something to come in, what is there must be displaced.**

**~Kemper Crabb**

Kemper says the overwhelming response to what he does is due to the preparation beforehand through prayer. "I speak to the ground below, breaking the curses of many generations. Then I speak to the atmosphere above, proclaiming the curse broken through Christ's sacrifice on the cross. When you deal with those things spiritually, people come to Christ so easily."

He says the more enjoyable instances of seeing the Spirit of God move in a powerful way is among the people where Kemper serves, those who are most needy, who know without a doubt their only hope is to trust in this God of whom Kemper speaks, a God who, though they are counted as lower than a flea in their culture, says they are priceless.

In 2014, during an inauguration of a new church in Jinja, Africa, Kemper saw a young girl crawling on the ground. She suffered from the most severe form of Spina Bifida.[32]

Just as he spoke to the sky above and earth below, Kemper spoke to the spirit of infirmity in the young girl, rebuking the illness. "Later, I looked over and she was dancing." Many of the local populace turned out for the event. At the end of the day, 870 had declared salvation through Christ.

In the telling, this process might sound simple, just a matter of faith and speaking redemption, but even in this Kemper has a bit of an advantage. He can *see* what most of us cannot. Spiritual forces, both good and evil, are clear to him.

Also, when God wants him to address/speak to a situation, Kemper will see what he calls a "vibration" in the spiritual realm. He describes this phenomenon as similar to what we would see when a heat wave shimmers on hot pavement. When he sees this vibration, he knows God is giving him the go-ahead to speak redemption. "Again," Kemper is quick to point out, "I do this out of obedience. This is not some trigger-happy thing."

This gets to the heart of what Kemper feels called to accomplish. The proper religious term? **Redemption**. Kemper likes to explain it as the apostle John does in Revelations, "Every tear shall be wiped away." (Rev. 21:4)

"It's a matter of speaking The Kingdom of Heaven as we go. You address the ground below and the atmosphere above, breaking every curse." He explains that the earth has a deep and varied spiritual history. Curses can be of a cultural, generational or even geographical nature. Regardless of

---

32 Also known as open spina bifida, myelomeningocele (pronounced: my-uh-loh-muh-NIN-juh-seel) is the form people usually mean when they use the term "spina bifida." In myelomeningocele, the baby's spinal canal remains open along several vertebrae in the lower or middle back. Because of this opening, both the membranes and the spinal cord protrude at birth, forming a sac on the baby's back. In some cases, skin covers the sac. Usually, however, tissues and nerves are exposed, making the baby prone to life-threatening infections. (Taken from The Mayo Clinic's spina bifida page: http://www.mayoclinic.com/health/spina-bifida)

a curse's source, Christ has won the victory over it. "As you do this, as you proclaim Christ's victory over every evil, it becomes like the Garden of Eden. When these spiritual strongholds are removed, then people are free to respond to the message of salvation."

He admits this process is an intense spiritual exercise that requires deep faith in God's authority. "It's about the most exhausting thing you can do."

This battle with the unseen is hard for our pragmatic society to accept. "The ones who need to hear and build their faith will," says Kemper. "The ones who can't accept that truth will scoff and ridicule. That's okay. But in the process, many hearts will burn to believe."

> "Curses can be of a cultural, generational or even geographical nature. When these spiritual strongholds are removed, then people are free to respond to the message of salvation."

**A Surprise Visit**

But even Kemper had to learn about and grow in this authority he has in Christ. He recalls the first time his ministry dove into the supernatural realm.

On a Texas Sunday afternoon in the 1970s, Kemper, who served as a deacon for his hometown Baptist church, was looking for the home of a church member who was sick. He got lost and approached a house to ask directions. When the woman who lived there heard he was from the local Baptist church, she pulled him inside to pray for her daughter who was in a coma.

As he prayed for the girl, it was clear to Kemper what needed to be done. However, what he was about to pray did not line up with the official doctrine of his church. “I rebuked the demon of infirmity that was in her. It came out. She sat up. Then later that day she asked Jesus into her heart.”

Did Kemper ever make it to the house he was supposed to visit? “I never *did* find it. But I was right where God wanted me to be,” he says with a smile.

### Dealing With the Demonic

In Kemper’s ministry, much of what he does involves the casting out of demons, a practice overlooked and even ridiculed in many churches. After all, we are a society that relies on medical and scientific intervention rather than ancient spiritual practices. Kemper points out that in scriptural accounts, Jesus spent 66% of his time driving out demons from their human hosts.

“I don’t need to convince folks in India, Africa and Asia that demons are real. The Juju, voodoo or dark magic is something they deal with all the time. When we rebuke those forces through Jesus, the people are freed.”

> MYSTERY OF THE KINGDOM #5:
>
> The casting out of demons: Everything that *is* has been created. In order for something to come in, what is there must be displaced.

UGANDAN JUJU (VOODOO) SITE WHERE
CHILD SACRIFICE IS PRACTICED EACH WEEK

To explain the issue of demons, Kemper starts by describing the root of the problem, once more delving into territory overlooked in most official church doctrine. "Most people who *do* believe in demons are under the impression these are fallen angels, but they're not. These are the spirits of the Nephilim, the half-man/half-angelic breed that first happened back before Noah's time." The angels who committed this offense, Kemper points out, were imprisoned and await judgment. However, their offspring remained, the reported "giants of old" who are mentioned on numerous occasions in the Old Testament. (See Gen. 6:4, Gen. 12:1, Gen. 13:7, Num. 13:17-33, and Josh. 12:4 for a biblical study of this theme.)[33]

Scripture says our struggle is not against flesh and blood but rather against principalities, powers, and the rulers of this present darkness (Eph. 6:12). Therefore, it's the spiritual side of things Kemper addresses first, in order for true metamorphosis to occur. As Kemper says, there needs to be a displacement in order for Christ to take up residence in a person's life. He refers to Matthew 12:28, **"If I cast out demons by the Spirit of God, *then* the Kingdom of Heaven has come unto you."**

Says Kemper, "Everything that *is* has been created. That's the first law of thermodynamics. In order for something to come in, something must be displaced."

This is why Kemper first addresses the spiritual climate when he inaugurates churches. "When people's minds and bodies are freed from these powers of demonic activity, then they can hear and receive salvation. They come so easily. It's like fruit falling off a tree."

Kemper credits this practice of speaking to evil, displacing it with Christ's authority and light, as the key to the success of his ventures. "This is why we've led 11 million to salvation in 30 years. This is why demoniacs are freed, people are healed and we've even had some raised from the dead. Very simply, Jesus said, 'All who believe in me, the works I do you will do. And you will do more.'" *(Kemper paraphrase of John 14:12)*

> "Jesus came to reverse the works of Satan. I love to teach that to the children."

33 For a good overview of this topic see: http://bible-truths-revealed.com/adv63.html & http://www.theforbiddenknowledge.com/hardtruth/giants2.htm

When teaching new believers, this opposition to evil is one of his top priorities. "To do this, we go back to simple scripture. Jesus came to reverse the works of Satan." Joy lights up Kemper's features. "I love to teach that to the children."

But he is also quick to point out that the emphasis, even with such powerful miracles, has to remain on the Kingdom of Heaven. "I'm very clear with folks that their salvation and healing is for *The Kingdom*, not for them. Also, just like Jesus told the disciples who came back raving, 'We cast out demons, we raised the dead, etc.' He said, 'Cool it. Rejoice that your name is written in the Lamb's Book of Life.'" *(Kemper paraphrase of Luke 10:20)*

Kemper says the redemption of creation includes the DNA of individuals, even when those individuals have a high percentage of what he calls "demonic DNA." "A man came to me a couple years ago who had an interest in Christianity but he had demonic DNA. (referring to the Nephilim bloodline mentioned before)—he even knew his lineage. The man said, 'There's some reason I can't believe but I really want to.'"

But Kemper had a deeper faith in Jesus' love than he did in the man's demonic heritage. "So I went back in this man's DNA, *before creation was*, and did what Jesus could do. I changed that DNA. You can do what Jesus did. All authority is given. Just like it says in Colossians, 'everything was made by him and through him and for him.'"[34]

The man prayed with Kemper and received Christ as Lord of his life.

Kemper pumps a fist in the air like a winning coach. "Yes! His name is written in the Book of Life."

34 "For in him all things were created: things in heaven and on earth, visible and invisible, whether thrones or powers or rulers or authorities; all things have been created through him and for him." Col. 1:16 NIV

# Chapter Twelve
## NECESSARY MIRACLES

**"There is *no way* we could do what we've done without applying the Mysteries of the Kingdom of Heaven."**

**Kemper Crabb**

How in the world can a retired coach afford, not only to travel to the other side of the world about five times a year, but also to supply operating funds to several hundred churches, orphanages, schools, plus a few seminaries and even hospitals? As stated before, Servants of the King applies 100% of incoming funds to ministry outreach. "No one gets a salary," Kemper reports. "Every penny goes to the work, to the children."

Thus Kemper and Servants of the King can accomplish much more with much less money. Kemper reports, "I can feed and clothe a child for about $2.40 a month."

But to accomplish so much, practically speaking, requires money, and lots of it. Where does it come from?

One of Kemper's major channels of funding is his buying and selling of precious gems. The idea came to him, he said, when he was on a plane flying home from India. "I thought, 'what does India have? Well, it has death, poverty, disease, orphans and lots of suffering. But it also has precious gems.'"

In that moment, Kemper heard God's guidance in his heart. *"Every child you save will be a precious gem in my crown."*

"It was all about redemption. I find precious gems and redeem them to alleviate suffering."

Thus the retired coach who had a few honorary doctorates, had been nominated three times for a Nobel Prize, and had a masters degree in science education and applied kinesiology, went back to school, undertaking the rigorous training to become a professional gemologist. "Now *that* was tough;" Kemper recalls, "much harder than anything I had studied before." But the intense training paid off. Kemper, with his ties to professional sports, held gemstone parties for professional football players and their wives. "They're used to nice things and they know I have the best. Plus they get the added satisfaction of knowing where their money's going." Kemper adds, "If ya haven't checked lately, building a hospital is expensive."

In regards to the orphanages that have been built through Servants of the King, Kemper reports he can run each of them, feeding and clothing the 40 or so children and even paying the teacher's salaries, for about 87 U.S. dollars per month. "I can do that," Kemper states. "I can sell a topaz or somethin'."

Gems are not the only source of regular provision for the work of Servants of the King. Kemper, always the entrepreneur, also utilizes a bit of Africa's abundant natural resources. He established and oversees a coffee plantation and tree farm. "The soil is so fertile," Kemper explains. "Whereas we might have a few inches of topsoil in the U.S, Africa has about sixty-five feet!"

Plus, when Kemper speaks at college ceremonies, churches, businessmen's meetings or any other function, he has the checks made out directly to

Servants of the King. "It works well," Kemper says. "They get a good write-off and children are cared for."

When on his mission excursions, he has to keep reminding those who work with him that just because his skin is white and he is a missionary does not mean he will live lavishly or spend money on expensive accommodations or meals.

Kemper avoids the type of missionary life where one lives in comfort and ease while the condition of the people he's there to help doesn't really change. "I call that type of mission work 'Ivory Tower missions.' I truly don't want to sound judgmental but that's the impression the native people in these third world countries often have. They come to us with their hand out because they expect us to flip 'em a quarter or somethin'."

A TYPICAL RURAL UGANDAN VILLAGE

This is why Kemper and Servants of the King establish a *covenant*[35] with the village churches. Yes, SOK provides the materials to build, but the

35 a divine contract--Mystery of the Kingdom #4

people who live there do the bulk of the work. The local church body also *covenants* to take care of the orphans and widows in their village. Says Kemper, "This is a partnership. There's no charity here. They work and their community is stronger for it."

SOK WORKERS PUT FINISHING TOUCHES ON A NEW UGANDAN VILLAGE CHURCH

Even though large sums of money pass through Kemper's hands each year, he continues to drive the same old pick-up truck, his clothing is simple, and he and his wife live in a modest home. When traveling, he's been known to sleep in his truck's small camper in order to save the price of a hotel.

In fact, his family has a running joke. Kemper's daughter Dawna says, "We tease him that he never has the price of a cup of coffee in his pocket."

Kemper's wife Tommye still works as a college professor. "After all," Kemper quips, "*somebody's* gotta make a living."

Kemper and Tommye in 2012. Kemper was awarded the Delta Tau Delta Distinguished Alumni Achievement Award. Photo credit, De Ann Hoeft, www.deannsphotographystudio.com

# Chapter Thirteen
## THOUGH HE SLAY ME

**"For to me to live is Christ, and to die is gain."**

**Phil. 1:21 KJV**

It was mid-December 2013. Kemper's daughter, Dawna, received a call from Calcutta. Her father was not doing well. His heart was racing. He was very fatigued. He was in a hospital in Calcutta and could not get an earlier flight home. She sent out the call to friends and family: Please pray.

Cell phones buzzed with scripture promises, prayerful declarations and hopeful words. Many wondered if Kemper was going home; if he would finally get to rejoice with the hundreds of children whose lives had ebbed away in his arms.

Finally, a couple days later, friends and family received great news. Kemper's heart rate had slowed. He was regaining strength. It appeared he was out of the woods.

In a phone call later that week, Kemper confessed his own fear, once more turning the trauma into a joke. "I thought for a while there they were gonna be sending me home in a box!"

But later, talking once more from the comfort of his home and back in the embrace of family, Kemper related yet another supernatural experience.

"Ya know in the scripture where they talk about those gates of Heaven that are fashioned from one giant pearl? Well I was there. My heart was just buzzing with joy and I wanted to stay so badly. But two angels blocked my way and pushed me back."

He paused, "I guess there's more for me to do."

And how did Kemper round out his near-death experience in India?

"When I was strong enough, we went out that night and rescued 25 more children. Isn't that neat?"

# THE PLAN OF SALVATION "EMPOLOGOMA STYLE"

When it comes to salvation, Kemper keeps things simple. He works with an interpreter to explain the importance of the Ten Commandments as God's template for how we, as followers of Christ, are called to live. The following is a rough transcript of one of Kemper's calls to salvation.

"When God told Moses to bring the Israelites out of Egypt, they didn't know how they were supposed to live. God gave Moses Ten Commandments. God Himself wrote these commandments in stone for Moses to give to the people. When the people heard them they said to Moses, 'We can't keep those commandments.' Moses said, 'You must.'

KEMPER AND UGANDAN SOK DIRECTOR PETER ISABIRYE LEAD AN INAUGURATION SERVICE

Here's where you find the power to do this. Ya don't have to go up into the heavens. Ya don't have to descend into the ground or cross over the sea. The power to keep the commandments is in your mouth.[36]

God told them to say His commandments every day, to study them, to talk about them and to inscribe them where they can read them. This is why we put a copy of the Ten Commandments on your church so everyone can read them.

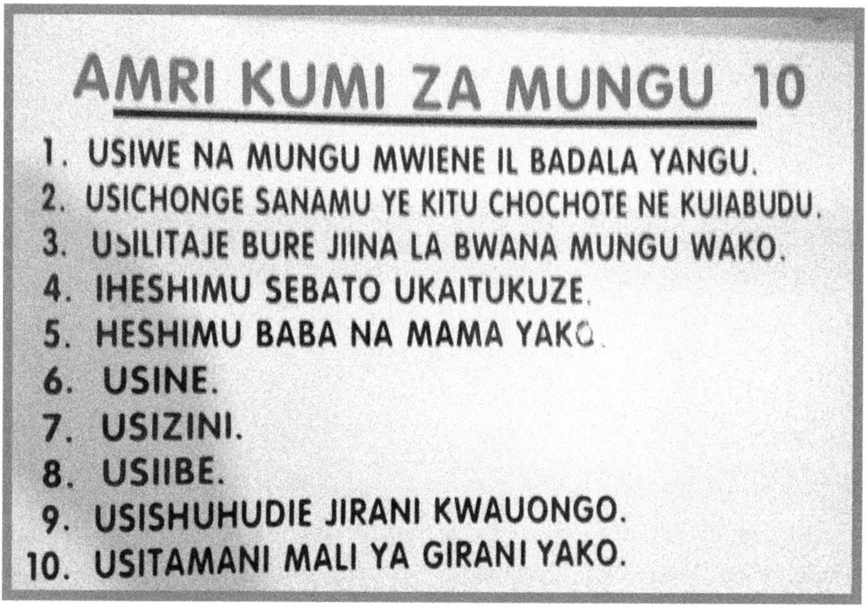

AMRI KUMI ZA MUNGU 10

1. USIWE NA MUNGU MWIENE IL BADALA YANGU.
2. USICHONGE SANAMU YE KITU CHOCHOTE NE KUIABUDU.
3. USILITAJE BURE JIINA LA BWANA MUNGU WAKO.
4. IHESHIMU SEBATO UKAITUKUZE.
5. HESHIMU BABA NA MAMA YAKO.
6. USINE.
7. USIZINI.
8. USIIBE.
9. USISHUHUDIE JIRANI KWAUONGO.
10. USITAMANI MALI YA GIRANI YAKO.

TEN COMMANDMENTS IN SWAHILI

"Also, there's a mystery of the Kingdom about covenants. When we pledge together before God to do something, this vow or promise is called a covenant. Will you covenant together with me to keep these commandments? Raise your hand if you're willing to do this.

"Now let's say these commandments together:

---

36 Refers to Deuteronomy 30:11-14 11Now what I am commanding you today is not too difficult for you or beyond your reach.12 It is not up in heaven, so that you have to ask, "Who will ascend into heaven to get it and proclaim it to us so we may obey it?"13 Nor is it beyond the sea, so that you have to ask, "Who will cross the sea to get it and proclaim it to us so we may obey it?" 14 No, the word is very near you; it is in your mouth and in your heart so you may obey it. (NIV)

#1 I will have no other gods before you.

#2 I will not worship any graven image.

#3 I will not take the Lord God's name in vain.

#4 I will remember the Sabbath Day and keep it holy.

#5 I will honor my father and my mother.

#6 I will not steal.

#7 I will not murder.

#8 I will not commit adultery.

#9 I will not tell lies.

#10 I will not covet what my neighbor has."

---

TEN COMMANDMENTS IN HINDI

After those gathered have repeated the Ten Commandments with him, Kemper continues with the profession for salvation as outlined in Romans 10 verse 9, that if we agree with Heaven with our mouth and speak that Jesus is Lord and profess our belief that God raised Him from the dead, we will be saved.

"The Bible says that the power of salvation is the same way. Ya don't have to go up into the heavens. Ya don't have to go down into the earth or cross over the sea. The power to be saved is in your mouth. If we confess with our mouth that Jesus is Lord and believe in our hearts that God raised Him from the dead, we shall be saved. So we're gonna do that all together now. If you want to receive Jesus as your Savior and Lord, repeat after me:

"I confess that Jesus is my Savior and my Lord. (The people repeat.)

"I believe in my heart that Jesus rose from the dead." (The people repeat.)

"I ask you, Lord Jesus, to be my Savior." (The people repeat.)

"Now how many of you said those words for the very first time?" (Hands go up.)

"Hallelujah!"

---

Kemper says the most glorious aspect of his ministry is when he leads people to salvation. "Ya see their eyes change," he says.

What does he mean by those words?

What Kemper describes is the change in expression when God's presence enters in. Faces that express confusion, suspicion, worthlessness, or simple curiosity transform to surprised joy.

As Kemper says, "I get to see that transformation happen to whole crowds of people right before my eyes."

A YOUNG GIRL PEEKS IN THE WINDOW DURING A CHURCH INAUGURATION CEREMONY

Kemper shakes his head in awe because, even after thirty-plus years, the miracle of Christ entering into the lives of those who profess Him as Savior and Lord still astounds him.

Kemper reiterates that, though miracles are wonderful, they are given by God to bring more souls into the Kingdom. They should never overshadow the true aim of salvation.

As an example, Kemper recalls what happened during a church meeting in Kenya in 2014. About sixty-two people had accepted Christ. One Muslim man refused. Kemper warned the Muslim man saying, "Sir, you're gonna burn in Hell." But God was not finished. Another man had just professed Christ as Lord and came up to shake Kemper's hand. The man reached out with his left hand because his right arm was withered. Kemper said, "No, I'm gonna shake your *right* hand." When Kemper shook the man's hand, the withered arm grew right there before everyone's eyes. As the people rejoiced, the Muslim man bowed before Kemper and said, "Sir, I do need Jesus as my Lord and Savior."

Kemper smiles with the vigor of a man half his age.

"That never, ever gets old."

A UGANDAN CHURCH INAUGURATION RIBBON-CUTTING CEREMONY

**Fellow Servants**

Through the years, many have joined Kemper on the mission field. They learn from the simplicity of his ministry, and carry on the vision of taking Christ to those who cannot give back. Here are a few recent reports from other Servants of the King.

1. Sandy Marek does follow up visits to churches that have been built by SOK. Summer of 2014 found her at twenty-four village churches in Uganda and three churches in island villages. She distributed Bibles and salvation bracelets to help the people learn more of the Gospel. During her six weeks in Africa, 2,141 proclaimed Christ for the first time. A large component of Sandy's outreach is showing

the *Jesus Film.*[37] Since so many have never read the Bible, this movie is often their first introduction to Christ's teachings. Sandy always offers a call to salvation at the close of the film. The response has been astounding.

2. Internet entrepreneur Jon Frendl traveled with Kemper to Africa in April of 2014. Jon says one of the most rewarding visits was to a church in Kenya that had been planted by Servants of the King about a decade before. "This was, truly, the healthiest church I've ever seen. There were hundreds of members of all ages. The congregation was so diverse and joyful. The fruit of vibrant spiritual growth was so abundant." So many salvations and miracles happened on the trip, Jon says it remains a bit of a blur. But his outlook will never be the same. "I'd been wanting to know God more; to have a deeper understanding. Meeting Kemper, hearing his stories, and then witnessing the ministry firsthand have opened my mind to the fact there is so much *more* of God than what we are taught in most churches."

3. In September of 2014, current Servants of the King President Kyle Coston led a team of five to Uganda, including his wife Cathi. Kyle reports, "During the fourteen days we were there, we visited ten churches and ten schools, preaching and teaching the Gospel of Jesus. More than 2,550 people proclaimed Jesus as their personal Savior. We also sent twenty-one children to school who were unable to afford it due to financial constraints."

---

37 The Jesus Film has been translated into more than 1,100 languages. Every day, an average of one person every eight seconds makes a decision to follow Christ due to this film. For more information on The Jesus Film Project go to: www.thejesusfilm.org

And the story continues with YOU. If you have never accepted Jesus as your Savior and Lord, there's no time like the present. As Kemper says, "Ya don't have to go up to the Heavens. Ya don't have to descend into the earth or cross over the sea. The power is simply in your mouth."

If you confess with your mouth that Jesus is Lord and believe in your heart that God raised Him from the dead, you SHALL be saved.

Please say this simple prayer aloud:

> "Dear Jesus,
>
> I confess with my mouth that you are the Son of God. I profess You as my Savior and Lord. I believe in my heart that You rose from the dead. Please come into my life. I give You all I am, all I will be. I even give you my past. From now on, I live and move and have my being in You.
>
> I pray all this in the holy name of my precious Savior Jesus.
>
> Amen."

As Kemper says, "Rejoice because your name is written!"

# SERVANTS OF THE KING

**Mission Statement:**

The mission of Servants of the King is the redemption of souls and alleviation of suffering throughout the world.

INDIA'S SNAKE CHARMERS

**Vision:**

1. Plant and build churches of all Christian denominations.

2. Assist established congregations of Christian faith in building brick sanctuaries on their own land with their own labor.
3. Create and maintain orphanages, schools, leprosariums and theological seminaries.
4. Create havens for widows, dying children, and people seeking the stories of Jesus Christ.

CHILDREN IN AFRICA OFTEN CARE FOR BABIES WHILE PARENTS WORK IN THE FIELDS

**Symbol:**

The Symbol used to represent Servants of the King was created by Kemper during SOK's inception. The X shape is the Celtic symbol for *Kang* which was used to represent *King*. Thus in Celtic writings, the X was used before a king's name. "The kings were called "Rex so-and-so," Kemper explains. "I simply put the *King* on the *Cross*."

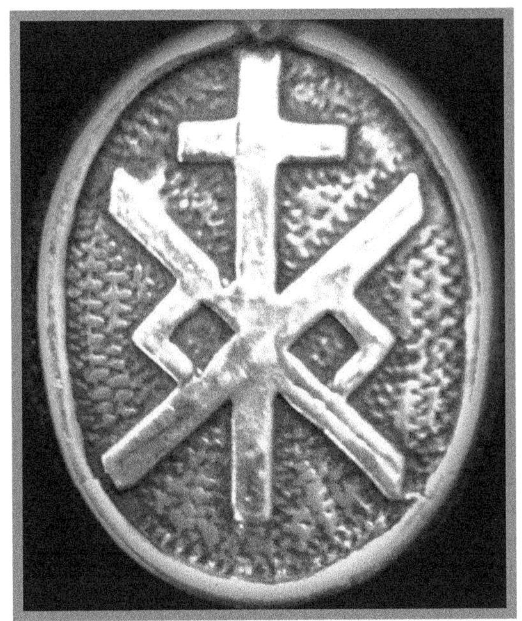

SERVANTS OF THE KING MEDALLION SHOWS THE "KANG" ON THE CROSS

**Goals:**

1. Build 6000 Christian churches in India:
2. Build 1000 Christian churches in Uganda:
3. Build 1500 Christian churches in South America
4. Drill and maintain water wells where necessary
5. Encourage the churches built with the backing of SOK to expand their missions to include orphanages, education and medical help for their communities.
6. Teach a curriculum of scripture but not denominational theology.
7. Orient ministry students to meet the needs of their home districts.

A NEW CHURCH ON INAUGURATION DAY--SUMMER 2014

**Accomplishments as of 2014:**

1. A grand total of 850 churches in India.

2. 904 churches in East Africa. Servants of the King is registered with Rwanda, Uganda, Tanzania, Kenya, and the Congo.

3. The vision for South America has just begun to be a reality. SOK now has 6 churches in Panama and in the northern part of Columbia.

4. Kemper says SOK includes water wells when needed. However, this does not overtake the first priority of saving souls.

5. The churches and orphanages built by SOK are intertwined in purpose and ministry. When a church is built, SOK provides funds for the care of orphans, but the congregants do the maintenance and treat the children as members of their family.

A UGANDAN VILLAGE BABY

6. The blind, lepers, and those with debilitating diseases are put in hospitals. SOK has built five leprosy hospitals (leprosariums), and two AIDS hospitals.

7. SOK has established thirty-six orphanages and 411 schools.

8. Since they need to provide pastors for the above ministries, SOK also built three seminaries. "We always emphasize, what was true in the Bible is true for us now. In a year we can cover the entirety of the Bible. They (the students) come to the seminary on Fridays & Saturdays weekly for a year. This teaching covers the Bible from Genesis to Revelations."

9. Seminary students are trained in their district so they can still do their duties, take care of their families, and then serve in their district.

10. Kemper states that SOK seminary teaching steers clear of denominational emphasis. "We don't teach 'doctrine.' We teach

the Bible with emphasis on 'God is the same yesterday, today and forever.'"

11. SOK Goals now: Says Kemper, "There's a bigger rush with the end coming and apocalypse drawing nigh. Sprinting is in order. Intensity is going toward more teaching of the people to take the gospel out to their neighbors themselves. We want our people in the churches to have a scriptural answer for the questions pagans will ask them, therefore we're training them on the presentation of the Gospel. This includes power and dominion over evil spirits."

**Frequently Asked Questions:**

1. How did SOK begin?

   Founder Kemper Crabb was called to India in the 1980s. After retiring from coaching, he began full time foreign missionary work in and around northern India. Servants of the King was begun to facilitate and broaden this work. SOK operates under the authority of the evangelical Episcopal Church. Kemper is an Episcopal priest and is also a member of a Baptist congregation in San Antonio, Texas.

2. What denomination of churches does Servants of the King build?

   SOK builds churches of all Christian faiths. They determine the denomination of the church by the contributor and the preference of those who will attend.

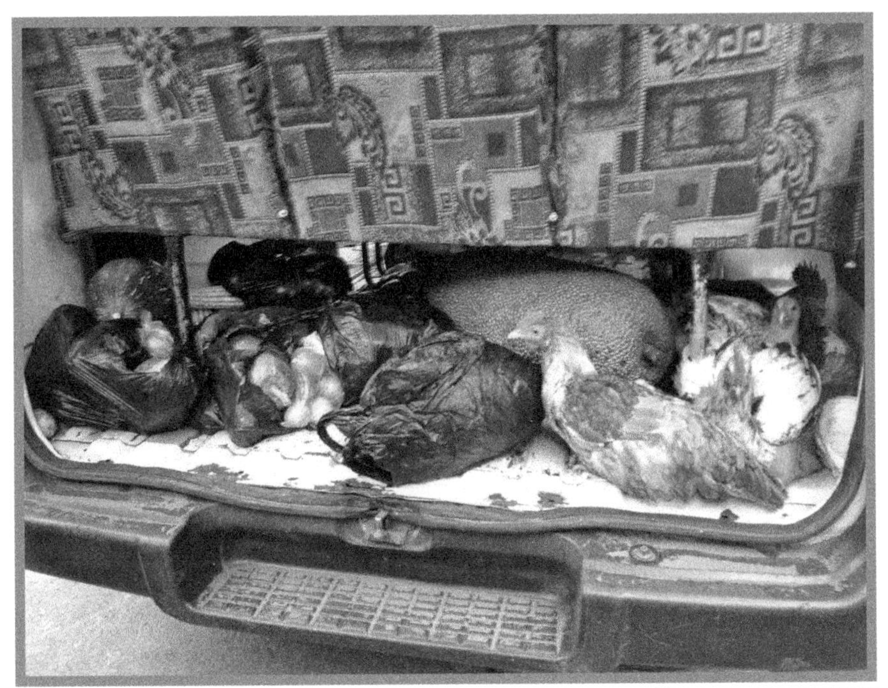

OFFERINGS BROUGHT BY UGANDAN VILLAGERS TO THANK GOD FOR THEIR NEW CHURCH FACILITY

3. What are SOK's Donation Use Guidelines?

Servants of The King has a completely different approach to using dollars contributed:

- All mission contributions go 100% to the mission program
- All overhead costs are separate donations designed specifically for this purpose
- No transportation or travel expenses are covered by the mission program
- Kemper receives NO salary, NO expense account, and NO reimbursements
- All connected with SOK contribute in time, talent, and/or money
- SOK members never ask for money

AFRICAN VILLAGE CHILDREN AT A CHURCH CELEBRATION

4. Why are Servants of the King churches painted blue and gold?

   It's a simple matter of practicality. Kemper says, "We got a good deal on lots of blue and gold paint once and just stuck with it."

# A WRITER'S VIEW

When it comes to Kemper Crabb, this surprisingly fit former coach with the southern twang, teasing manner and unassuming servant's persona who has some amazing stories to tell—remarkable stories of biblical proportions—one has to make a decision pretty quick. But as Kemper himself is prone to say, echoing the Apostle Paul, "If you don't believe me, believe me for my works sake." And echoing the words of Jesus, "You will know a tree by the fruit it bears."

So let's review our options in a logical, C.S. Lewis manner. Kemper Crabb is either:

a) A liar

b) A lunatic

c) Who he says he is

Upon meeting Kemper, the middle option is removed within two minutes of hearing him speak. His is a razor-sharp mind that, like a master computer, retrieves data from his eight-plus decades of living, reciting snatches of poetry, describing names, faces, shared jokes and shared pain with precision.

KEMPER RECEIVES MATOKE (PLAINTAINS), HIS LEAST-FAVORITE AFRICAN FOOD, AS A JOKE ON HIS 83RD BIRTHDAY FROM UGANDAN SOK DIRECTOR, PETER ISABIRYE

But could he be a liar, a shrewd huckster tricking susceptible followers to hand over their life savings for false aims or convincing them to bestow honor for feats he's never accomplished? Again, the evidence to the contrary is immense: the newspaper clipping showing him walking with Mother Teresa, the photos of numerous churches and orphanages, all painted his trademark blue and gold, a faithful wife of six decades, children, grandchildren and great grandchildren who are upstanding, dedicated members of society who attest to the veracity of his claims, honorary degrees and awards from his alma mater, Sam Houston State University, for being a highly decorated and distinguished alum. Plus—here's the kicker—he never asks for money. His missionary excursions are primarily self-funded.

AN EARLY PHOTO OF GRANDSON SCHEDEL WHO HAS ACCOMPANIED KEMPER ON MISSION TRIPS TO INDIA AND AFRICA SINCE HE WAS TWELVE YEARS OLD

But wait. If we're approaching this logically and our only other option is to believe that Kemper Crabb is exactly who he says he is.

- He has been guided from childhood by heavenly music
- God's faithful angels protect him, bring him encouragement, guidance and take direction from him in recognition of Jesus, the Christ, who dwells within him.
- He has been beaten, stoned, tortured, marked for murder, and imprisoned on numerous occasions.
- He has held hundreds of dying children in his arms as they drew their last breath.
- He laughed with and worked side-by-side with Mother Teresa who nominated him for a Nobel Peace Prize.
- In his thirty years of outreach in India, Africa and China, he has led more than 11 million to salvation in the name of Jesus.
- He has overseen and inaugurated thousands of community churches, schools, orphanages, and even several hospitals, leprosariums, and seminaries through his non-profit ministry, Servants of the King.

If we accept the above as fact, (which only scratches the surface of this amazing man's experiences) then we have a new paradigm to embrace. It's a worldview where a common Christian takes God at His word, does the works Christ did on Earth and, with constant peril to life and limb, uses the years he has been given to spread joy and light in the darkest of venues, living a life reminiscent of the prophet Elijah or the Apostle Paul—both the glories and the pain.

THE EARLY YEARS OF MINISTRY IN INDIA

For his entire life, Kemper has kept a low profile and has tried to give the honor for his accomplishments to others in order to, as he says, "stay below the radar" and even protect his family and co-workers from the ramifications of his deeds. He firmly believes, and is living proof, that one can accomplish so much more by dodging notoriety.

But the day came, as he boarded a plane for another mission excursion, that a heavenly messenger met him to relay a new directive.

**"Heavenly servant, it is time to tell your story."**

That's where I came in. In 2012 my family and I met Kemper Crabb. We marveled at his stories. Friends had brought me into the mix to see if I might be interested in writing Kemper's book. Interested? Extremely. Qualified? Gulp.

I recorded hours of Kemper's stories over the course of several interviews and even got acquainted with his lovely wife and family at their home in Texas. In the summer of 2014, my daughter and I accompanied Kemper throughout Uganda, Africa. What an honor to soak in the everyday miracles God works through His servant.

I remain astounded at the opportunity to befriend and pester Kemper and his family with unending questions. Will I ever feel worthy or qualified? Never. But our wonderful Heavenly Father has more in store for His children than we could ever ask or imagine.

I pray this book has transformed your perception of what is possible when we commit all to serving Christ. Furthermore, I pray for many more Kempers to rise, take up their cross, and serve God without reservation wherever He leads.

Aiming to be a Servant of the King,
Chana Keefer

CHANA & DAUGHTER MCKENNA IN UGANDA, AFRICA, 2014

## A Small Sample of the Hundreds of Churches built by Servants of the King since 1985

1 13:4

A Ugandan village church before SOK assistance

SOK church under construction

Church before SOK workers finish with paint and the Ten Commandments above the door

# ABOUT KEMPER CRABB

Kemper Crabb is founder of Servants of the King, a 501 (c)(3) charitable organization. Since 1985, SOK has built Christian churches, schools, hospitals, orphanages, leper care, and has assisted other mission workers proclaiming the Gospel of Jesus Christ in Asia and Africa.

www.servantsoftheking.org

# ACKNOWLEDGEMENTS

The author owes a debt of gratitude to so many who made the completion of this work possible. First, thank you Kemper and Tommye Crabb for opening your lives and home. Thank you Schedel and Dawna for ongoing support and manuscript reviews. Martha White, though I've never met you, your input has been invaluable. Many thanks to the Worship Factory Team: Kempton Bryan, Rod Shrekengost, Sue Stewart, Monique Donnelly, Jon Bryan and Mariana Goncalves (soon to be Bryan!) for introductions. Thank you Stormye Van Dyke for being such a vital link in God's plan. Jessica Schulman, you know what you did last summer. Cathi Coston, we're forever in your debt for recommending we add duct tape to our African necessities list. Peter and Prossey Isabirye, we love our African family! Photographer extraordinaire and pictoral archivist De Ann Hoeft, truly couldn't have done this without you. Jon and Hannah Frendl, you are encouragers in time of need. Mark, Micah, McKenna, Sky and Madeline, you are this author's haven. Thank you Real Life Church, RLC's Prayer Team, the Facebook 30/30 Prayer Group, and the Friday Night Pizza/Movie crew for sharing life. Yvonne Parks at PearCreative.ca, thank you again for loaning your phenomenal skills to cover design and interior layout. Thank you, Terri Keefer, for your timely photo clean-up assistance. Holly Van Houten, you are an editing whiz! Hugs and blessings on the Vowell and Keefer families for a life foundation that keeps on giving.

Huge thanks to Servants of the King supporters, workers, missionaries, orphans, lepers, seminary staff, students, and every life past, present and future, connected to this great work.

Finally, all glory to Our Heavenly Father, His precious Word made flesh, and His Holy Spirit for being the true Author and Finisher, Alpha and Omega, the Beginning and End. Amen.



All proceeds from the sale of this book go to the ongoing ministry of Kemper Crabb and Servants of the King.

# BONUS: SERVANTS OF THE KING SPIRITUAL WARFARE TRAINING

Before Kemper allows anyone to accompany him on the mission field with Servants of the King, he insists they undergo spiritual warfare training. What follows is a transcription of his teaching and the scriptural references on which he bases his effective use of Christ's authority over the forces of darkness. These principles have been utilized and proven effective through more than four decades of fruitful ministry.

The following is a compilation of notes taken from the teachings of missionary Kemper Crabb, founder of Servants of the King.

www.servantsoftheking.org

Arranged with comments by R. L. Chastain

Transcribed and edited for publishing by Chana Keefer

# SCRIPTURAL FOUNDATIONS *for* SPIRITUAL AUTHORITY IN MINISTRY

SPIRITUAL WARFARE TRAINING

"Don't waste time on things not of the Kingdom of God."

KEMPER CRABB

# SCRIPTURAL FOUNDATIONS FOR SPIRITUAL AUTHORITY IN MINISTRY

## *Spiritual Warfare Training*

Spiritual warfare is POSITIONAL CHRISTIANITY. When you realize where you sit (Eph. 2: 5-6 ***"But God, who is rich in mercy... raised us up together, and made us sit together in the heavenly places in Christ Jesus."***), then you know the authority by which you do spiritual warfare. You are seated with Him in heaven (spiritually), and the authority that you operate in is His authority. He said in Matthew 28:18, ***"All authority has been given to Me in heaven and on earth."*** As it is stated in Acts 17:28, ***"for in Him we live and move and have our being..."*** It is while you are 'moving, living and having your being' in Him that you are TOTALLY committed to Him. If you are totally committed to Him, then you will begin to learn to rightly discern the Word (2 Tim 2:15). Without discernment of the Word and the voice of God, you will place yourself in a position to be ministering out of the soul, addressing the wrong issue, teaching false doctrine, or creating a problem where there was previously no problem.

If you desire to be in a correct position with Him, then Matthew 6:33 must be a major desire in your heart and be made manifest in your life. Jesus said, ***"Seek you first the Kingdom of God and His righteousness."*** When your desire is to please Him (John 8:29) first and foremost, then as you seek Him and the reality of the Kingdom being made manifest in your life, He will hear you (John 10:27 ***"My sheep hear My voice, and I know them, and they follow Me."***) As you diligently seek Him and His Kingdom authority, the manifest reality (which is judged by its permanency as opposed to temporality), becomes evident as you begin to discern between the Kingdom of Light and the kingdom of darkness. This discernment between the Light and the darkness is essential if you are going to walk in His Kingdom authority.

***"But I tell you truly, there are some standing here who shall not taste death till they see the Kingdom of God."*** (Luke 9:27). Luke wrote in 17:21, ***"For indeed, the Kingdom of God is within you."*** The Kingdom of God is here and now. It is powerful and active and its authority is available to those who desire to make King Jesus their King. To be a servant of a king, you must yield up ALL of your desires, rights and privileges to the authority and wishes of the king. Therefore, to be a servant of the King Lord Jesus, you must not only yield all of those things to Him, but your commitment to Him must be born out of a life-consuming LOVE for Him. His call to you was not first "DO," but rather, "If you LOVE me..." then He said, "KEEP My commandments" (teachings). Life-consuming love will bear much fruit that shall remain and the Father will be glorified by it. (John 15:8)

If we are seated (spiritually) in Christ Jesus, on His throne, then there must be changes that take place in our natural life which are made manifest and apparent to all who are associated with us in the daily routine of life. Paul wrote to the Romans (8:29) that we were to be ***"... conformed to the image of His Son..."*** The Greek word for "image (elkon 1504) always assumes a prototype, that which it not merely resembles but from which it is drawn." (Strong's lexical Aids). Made in His image, conformed to His image is not just an appearance or resemblance of, but it involves actually being like Him. We become "bone of His bone and flesh of His flesh." We are to be a bodily representation of the Lord Jesus. Our life should mirror or reflect His life. We must say as Jesus said, ***"I come to do YOUR WILL, O GOD..."*** (Hebrews 10:9). We should have "clean hands and a pure heart" and our desire should be only towards Him in pleasing service (not duty).

When Peter asked Jesus as to what the Apostle John was going to do, Jesus replied it was really of no concern to Peter. Jesus replied, ***"... if I will that he tarry till I come, what is that to you?"*** And then came the admonition: ***"... follow me."*** (John 21:22). To 'follow' Him meant, not just walking along behind Him, but rather to do what He was doing and say what He was saying. We are to be His voice, His healing and delivering hands, His authority in calling those things that are not as though they were." (Romans 4:17b). In essence, we are to do the same work that Jesus did: ***"I only say what I hear the Father speaking and do what I see Him doing."***

While we fret and worry about the events of life and try to solve the many problems of daily living, Jesus said that He was not of this world kingdom. In John 18:36, He stated, ***"My Kingdom is not of this world."*** He was IN this world kingdom but He was not controlled or manipulated by it. Jesus, in speaking to His disciples concerning Satan said, ***"... he has nothing in Me."*** (John 14:30). Satan had no control or authority over Jesus because He knew the will of the Father and He had set His heart's desires and intents on always pleasing the Father in everything that He said or did.

The Word tells us that the "natural" man cannot understand or receive what the Spirit of God says or has to offer. 1 Corinthians 2:14 explains it this way: ***"But the natural man receives not the things of the Spirit of God: for they are foolishness to him: neither can he know them, because they are spiritually discerned."*** Until a person is born-again (born from above or of God), he is incapable of understanding those things that relate to the Kingdom of Heaven because they are beyond understanding with the natural intellect. Our soul has intellect, doctrine, and theory but the spirit in man has revelation and knows the Lord and understands the working of His Spirit—the Holy Spirit.

According to Acts 17:28, we are to ***"live and move and have our being in Him"*** and this is done by the work of the Holy Spirit in and through us. As we have the "mind of Christ," we are led by the Spirit and the life of King Jesus is made manifest through us in our daily lies. We know and understand that the eternal things and those things that are of profit to us are not of the flesh but spirit. John 6:63 has this to say about the Spirit: ***"It is the spirit that quickens (makes alive); the flesh profits nothing; the words that I speak unto you, they are spirit and they are life."*** We must be able to understand and operate in the spiritual arena and not only in our own intellectual and sense capacity. Reality is judged by its permanency; those things which are eternal. We live and operate in the temporal most of the time and have very little knowledge of the eternal.

In Luke 4:18-19, we find Jesus explaining to the people concerning the work and the power of the Holy Spirit. He said, ***"The Spirit of the Lord is upon me, because He has anointed me to preach the gospel to the poor; He has sent Me to heal the broken-hearted, to preach deliverance to the captives and recovering of sight to the blind, to set at liberty them that are bruised, to preach the acceptable year of the Lord."*** Through His authority and the power of the Holy Spirit, Jesus: preached to the poor, healed, delivered, restored sight to blind eyes, and set at liberty those who are bruised (oppressed), and preached about the acceptable year of the Lord. These are the things that the Lord anointed Him with the Holy Spirit to do, and these are the same things that He said we should do. In John 14:12, we read where Jesus told His disciples, ***"Verily, verily, I say to you, he that believes on Me, the works that I do shall he do also; ... because I go to My Father."***

In 1 John 3:8 we read, ***"He that commits sin is of the devil; for the devil sinned from the beginning. For this purpose the Son of God was manifested, that He might destroy the works of the devil."*** What works did Jesus do that He said we were to do? Matthew 4:23 addresses this issue: ***"And Jesus went about all Galilee, teaching in their synagogues,***

***and preaching the gospel of the kingdom, and healing all manner of sickness (spiritual in nature), and all manner of disease (pathological in origin) among the people."*** When we read the accounts of Jesus' works, He spent two-thirds of His time casting out demons. This was what Jesus said that we were to do also: heal the sick and diseased, cast out demons, preach the Kingdom of God, and teach the people. He said that we were to go and make disciples. He did not say that we were to go and win the lost, but rather make "disciples." If we only get the people saved or "born again," that would be tantamount to birthing a natural baby and wishing it good luck and then walking off and leaving it to fend for itself. Newborn "babes in Christ" do not have the knowledge or ability to stand against the wiles and destruction of Satan who has only one agenda, ***"to steal, kill and destroy."*** (John 10:10a).

The fact that He said that "You Shall" do these things is not a matter of debate but rather of obedience. When the King gives a command, does the servant have the right to say, "I don't think that I want to do that. I don't completely understand and besides, I really don't feel like doing it. That would be too embarrassing to me?" When did the Bride get the revelation that she was god and knew exactly what and how her life should be run? When did the servant become greater than the master or the one who goes become greater than the one who sends? When did you and I become the god-king of our own lives and God become our servant? Who instructs the Creator of the Universe on how to run the universe? Where were we when He created the heavens and the earth or split the sea for Israel, caused there to be seasons of the year, or created life from a seed? ***"You shall do these things."*** Are we? If we have not been doing what Jesus did, why not? *If you do not care whether or not you haven't been doing them, then why are you reading this? Save your time, spend it on yourself and don't add more accountability to yourself because you have now heard more TRUTH: truth that you are now responsible to act upon and be either blessed or cursed according to your decision.*

May the Creator of Heaven and earth give us understanding, remove all scales of blindness from our eyes and dullness from our hearing that we may know and understand the heart, desires, and workings of the God of

Heaven and earth. He is the One who paid a price, beyond our greatest imagination and experience, that in our receiving His gift of Life, Jesus the Christ, we might have life everlasting in His kingdom. His Kingdom is a kingdom of Light, while the kingdom we create is a kingdom of darkness. We can't walk in light and darkness, or serve two masters.

In this world, there are supernatural forces at work all of the time. Everything that is done on this earth involves the presence of spirits, either good or evil. It has been that way since Satan was cast out of heaven because of his pride and desire to be god. If we have ever wondered why or how someone could do or say a certain thing, good or bad, it was because of the influence of spirits on their mind. Having the Word, the mind of Christ in our heart and memory, will enable us to make the right decisions and keep us from willfully entering into sin. It is for this reason that we are told to ***"pray without ceasing."*** (1 Thess. 5:17). When we learn to walk in an attitude of prayer and communication with the Father at all times, then we will be in constant contact with the Father and we will be able to ***"live and move and have our being in Christ."*** As we ***"submit to God, the devil will flee from us."*** (James 4:7). Our power or ability to walk a holy walk in this life comes from knowing the Word of God, the Author of the Word, understanding your authority from the Word, and walking in obedience to Him and His Word. ***"Obedience is better than sacrifice,"*** (1 Samuel 15:22). It is much easier to "sacrifice" than to be obedient. The only problem is that our sacrifices usually are not sacrifices at all but rather an inconvenience. The emphasis should be put on the obedience rather than on the sacrifice. If we are concentrating on the sacrifice instead of the obedience then we have already missed the point of the statement.

When we stay in contact with the Kingdom of Heaven and are listening to the King, then we will be doing the same things that the King did when He was on earth. Matthew 4:23 tells us what our Lord did: ***"and Jesus went about all Galilee Teaching in their synagogues and Preaching the gospel of the Kingdom, and Healing all manner of Sickness and all manner of Disease among the people."*** Matthew 9:35 is an almost word-for-word repeat of 4:23. He went about doing the work of the

Kingdom and destroying the works of the devil. The destruction of the works of darkness allows the Kingdom of Heaven's light to be made manifest on the earth, in and through the lives of individuals.

Jesus did not come to promote the church, but rather the Kingdom of God. It is for the church to proclaim the Kingdom by saying and doing what Jesus did. Jesus laid down His life and offered up His blood as a once-and-for-all sacrifice for the redemption of the church; that being redeemed, it should proclaim the Kingdom of God to a lost, dying and hurting world. Why should the gates of hell not prevail against the church? Because the church is the means through which the Lord has chosen to attack the works of darkness and destroy them that the people might be delivered and set free.

The Israelites had to apply the blood of a spotless lamb to the doorposts of their houses in order to be delivered from death as the death angel passed over Egypt. Death came to the houses that did not have blood on their doorposts, regardless of their standing in the world kingdom; whether rich or poor, famous or infamous, death was no respecter of rank or social standing. The same is true of us today. If the blood of The Lamb of God, Jesus, has not been applied to our life (by faith) as a sacrifice for our sin, then death will come to us and we shall be separated from the presence of God and the Kingdom of Light and Life for eternity. Freedom from the bondage, death and destruction of the devil was not cheap. It cost our Lord Jesus *everything.* He gave up everything that those who had nothing might be made rich. 2 Corinthians 8:9 puts it this way: ***"For you know the grace of our Lord Jesus Christ, that, though He was rich, yet for your sakes He became poor, that you through His poverty might be rich."*** The riches that He provided, however, were far more than money; they were the riches of the Kingdom of Heaven that we might walk in them and do what He did by the same authority that He walked in while He was on the earth.

1 Peter 2:9 proclaimed that we, as children of God, are part of a chosen generation. ***"But you are a chosen generation, a royal priesthood, a holy nation, a peculiar people; that you should show forth the praises***

***of Him who has called you out of darkness into His marvelous light."*** God has chosen a people from out of the earth, a people who love Him more than this world or their own selves; people who would be so thankful for what He has done for them that they offer up their own lives to Him in adoration, praise and obedient service. We are called a priest. A priest was a mediator between God and the people. He went to the Lord on behalf of the people and then he revealed what the Lord had said concerning the people and His desires for them. The pastor, our shepherd, is to stay in the Word and before the Father on our behalf and to know His heart's desire for us. It is not his job to run the church organization but rather to make sure that true, holy, God-fearing, and respecting disciples are being raised up to do those things that Jesus did. The church is an organism, not an organization. It is alive, not a group of functions, rules, and regulations to be managed as one would a business.

Our Heavenly Father did not leave us to make it on our own. He provided apostles, prophets, and evangelists, and pastors, and teachers (Ephesians 4:11). ***"For the perfecting (maturing) of the saints, for the work of the ministry, for the edifying of the body."*** In other words, He made provision for us to be equipped to do the work of Jesus.

The Lord did not just all of a sudden decide to pick out some people to serve Him as His representatives on earth, in the Kingdom of Heaven. We read in Romans 8:29 that He had planned this time and selected those to serve Him, out of love, from the foundation of the world. This is from the Amplified Edition: ***"For those whom He foreknew—of whom He was aware and loved beforehand—He also destined from the beginning to be molded into the image of His Son (and share inwardly His likeness). That He might become the firstborn among many brethren."***

Being conformed is a choice on our part to allow ourselves to be changed, molded into something different, not an act on His part to make us different. Our conformity is to His life, not a set of rules, philosophies, traditions, or doctrines whereby we must work to become something. If we are to be conformed to His life, then it means that *we must live* as Christ did. Impossible, you say? Well, not according to the Word of God. Philippians 2:5 says, ***"Let this mind be in you which was also in Christ Jesus,"*** states that we are to have the same mind that Christ had. Galatians 2:20 makes this comment: ***"I am crucified with Christ: nevertheless I live, yet not I, but Christ lives in me."*** It is not our life but the life of Christ being made manifest through us in our daily living. It is about Him healing, delivering, comforting, and blessing through you and me. It is NOT about us doing anything. It is about Him doing it through us, and in this way He gets all the glory.

Matthew 6:33 explained what we are to be about: ***"Seek you first the Kingdom of God and His righteousness, and all these things shall be added unto you."*** It is first the Kingdom, His Kingdom, that we seek, then everything will follow. It is what He is about doing and saying, in Kingdom authority, that we are to seek, that those same things that He did should be taking place in our lives also. Simply put, when others look at us, they should see the character, love, and all that He was about, flowing out of our lives (including doing the same things that He did).

In John 14:11 Jesus said, ***"Believe Me that I am in the Father and the Father is in me: or else believe Me for the very works' sake. Verily, verily I say to you, He that believes on Me, the works that I do shall he do also and greater works than these shall he do; because I go to My Father."*** We are to be doing the very same works that Jesus did. The Creator God spoke and things happened. We have all the authority that Jesus had. We should have the same vision that He had, the vision of God the Father. Our vision should be *his* vision, not ours that is based upon emotions, human reasoning and knowledge, or need.

In order for us to walk in His authority, we must always be in touch with Jesus. Our desires should not only be the same as His, but they should be His desires. ***"I do always those things which please the Father."*** Well, what is the Father doing? Healing, delivering, saving, blessing, comforting, guiding, loving, giving, and the list goes on and on. Obviously, we can't do all these things, but we know the One who can and He has called us to be His body, hands, feet, and mouth in the earth—bringing about the manifesting of the Kingdom of Heaven.

If Satan is not releasing trouble into your path, then you may be going the wrong way. Why? Because when we walk in the same way, and do the same things that Jesus did, we will find trouble cropping up and trying to stop us. Matthew 28:18-20 reads, ***"And Jesus came and spoke to them saying, 'All power is given to Me in heaven and in earth. Go therefore and teach all nations, baptizing them in the name of the Father, and of the Son, and of the Holy Spirit: Teaching them to observe All things whatsoever I have commanded you.'"*** When we begin to do all things that Jesus did and commanded us to do, the kingdom of darkness is definitely going to get upset and begin trying to stop what we are doing by any means; evil doesn't play fair or by rules other than to steal, kill, and destroy. (John 10:10a)

Mark 16:17 reads this way: ***"And these signs shall follow…"*** Satan doesn't want to see "signs" occurring and he will try to interfere with or stop these things from happening. He doesn't want to see the Kingdom of Heaven being made manifest because he knows that the gates of hell shall not prevail against it. He will try to stop the progress and manifestation of the Kingdom and there are three things that will stop it:

1) Comfort

2) We've never done it this way

3) Organization.

First, we are seldom willing to give up our comfort; we want things to look and feel good… acceptable. We certainly are not expected to do any thing that might bring disfavor, reproach, or ridicule upon us!

Secondly, if we haven't been doing it that way, then we certainly can't go against tradition. Why, what would others say about us if we strayed from tradition? They may even think that we were radical or a heretic and we MUST preserve our reputation (even though Christ did not make one or himself. Philippians 2:7).

And then, we must not forget to organize! If we can't seem to walk in His Spirit and see signs and wonders occurring regularly, the only wonder is that the Lord doesn't destroy us all because we immediately begin trying to manufacture signs. Rather than walk in and by the power of the Holy Spirit, we try to create signs, wonders and miracles. We have read the book so we should be able to cause things to happen *some way!*

However, signs and wonders do not occur where unbelief reigns. 2 Corinthians 4:3-4 reads, ***"But if our gospel be hid, it is hid to them that are lost; in whom the god of this world has blinded the minds of them which believe not."*** Before those who have been blinded by the god of this world can see, hear and understand, the blindness and deafness must be rebuked by the authority of Jesus Christ, (which authority you have as a believer).

James 4:6-7 declares that: ***"... (God) gives grace to the humble."*** And we must humble ourselves, ***"Submit yourselves therefore to God. Resist the devil and he will flee from you. Draw near to God and He will draw near to you..."*** As we submit and draw near to God, the devil will flee. On the other hand, if we have darkness in our lives, it is an open door for demon influence to enter since Satan is the ruler of darkness. Darkness is his kingdom and he has authority in darkness. Just as the Kingdom of Heaven is the Kingdom of Light, so Satan's kingdom is a kingdom of darkness. The Bible declares that if the light in our eyes is darkness, how great will that darkness be! (Matt. 6:23)

Another thing to remember is that God has no time limit on His agenda; only man puts time limits on what he is doing. God is not bound by time. Man operates and lives in time. (John 14:30) Jesus, speaking to His disciples, said, ***"... for the prince of this world is coming and has nothing in Me."*** Satan had absolutely no control over Jesus. There was not any area of Jesus' life that Satan had any control or authority over. Jesus Christ was in complete control of every area of His life. Even in His death, He was in control because He said, ***"... Father, into Your hands I commend my spirit..."*** (Luke 23:46). No one took His life from Him, He offered it up as a sacrifice, willingly, to the Father on our behalf. No man took His life from Him. Rather He OFFERED it as a sacrifice for man's salvation.

In our Gethsemane (oil press), if we pass through victorious (as did our Lord), then our cry to the Father will be, "Not my will but Yours be done." If in view of what we must face on behalf of the Kingdom, we uncompromisingly, fervently, with diligence press on, we will find that Satan has 'no part' in us. The strain and intensity of Gethsemane is so great, that a half-hearted commitment will never stand the test; we will walk away in defeat. Those who have been chosen, and because of that call, have said emphatically "Yes," will find that the forces of evil will pull out all the stops in order to derail their pursuit of the life of Christ being made manifest through their vessel of clay that ALL of the glory will go to Him. An intimate relationship with the Father through our King Jesus causes panic in the kingdom of darkness because those forces know that the power and authority of Christ is about to be released against the darkness. Satan has NO authority over King Jesus in us and it is this relationship that he wants to destroy, not just cause us to commit some sin. Repentance will take care of the sin, but if the life of Christ Jesus is nullified in us, then a great victory for the darkness in this world has just been won. Be very careful to remain (abide) IN King Jesus that His life may abide in you because in The Light is no darkness. Give no place for sin to remain in you. Only you have the choice of allowing or disallowing sin into your daily living (which includes your thoughts as well as those things you desire.)

1 John 5:19, ***"We know that we are of God, and the whole world lies in the power of the evil one (wickedness)."*** This is part of the reason why we are told to, ***"... not be conformed to the world but rather be transformed by the renewing of your mind that you may prove what is that good, and acceptable, and perfect will of God."*** (Romans 12:2). We will operate under the power of the one to whom we choose to say 'Yes,' whether good or evil, light or darkness, righteousness or unrighteousness, holiness or perversion. As Joshua told the people of Israel, ***"Choose you this day whom you will serve."***

Isaiah 61:1,2 ***"The Spirit of the Lord God is upon Me; because the Lord has anointed Me to preach good tidings to the meek; He has sent Me to bind up the brokenhearted, to proclaim liberty to the captives and the opening of the prison to them that are bound; to all that mourn; to appoint to them that mourn in Zion, to give to them beauty for ashes, the oil of joy for mourning, the garment of praise for the spirit of heaviness; that they might be called the tree of righteousness, the planting of the Lord, that He might be glorified."*** Beauty for ashes refers to depression, which is a spirit, and there is a need to be delivered from it. While the spirit and the soul may be saved, the mind and body are still open to attack from evil spirits. It is for this reason that we need to have discernment in order to know the source when we are attacked, whether it is spiritual, physical, or emotional.

1 Kings 22: 21, 22, ***"And there came forth a spirit, and stood before the Lord and said, I will persuade him (Ahab). And the Lord said to him, "Wherewith?" And he said, "I will go forth, and I will be a lying spirit in the mouth of all his prophets." And He said, "You shall persuade him, and prevail also; go forth and do so."*** Because of the attitude of Ahab's heart, the Lord sent a lying spirit to his prophets so that they would tell him what he wanted to hear. This is why we are told to "try" or test the spirits to see where they originate… Light or darkness, God or Satan, or our own desires and imagination.

In Mark 11:12-26, Jesus cursed the fig tree because it appeared to have fruit but it did not. There are fig trees in the Christian community who have the appearance of fruit bearing, with good-sounding words and prayers. Jesus spoke to the issue all of the time and we need to do the same as He did. When we speak, we should speak the Word and the words that we hear the Father speaking, in faith, just as Jesus did. We should not speak words just because it may sound good or be appropriate, but we should speak only His words. When we address an issue, we should speak in His authority in Jesus' name—blessings or curses.

Deuteronomy 30:10-14: ***"If you hearken to the voice of the Lord your God, to keep His commandments and His statutes which are written***

***in this book of the law, and if you turn to the Lord your God with all your heart and with all your soul. This commandment is not far from you… But the Word is very near to you, in your mouth, and in your heart, that you may do it."*** The Word never changes and it is a blueprint for us to live by. The Word is the same as Jesus Christ; the same yesterday, today, and forever. It never changes. Turning to the Lord and offering our heart, soul, mind, and body to Him to use as He desires, will keep us in a close, intimate, loving relationship.

The Word is in our mouth and we must confess it continually, every day. It is releasing the Kingdom of Heaven into the earth and against the gates of hell that the Bride of Christ may walk in freedom from fear and oppression brought against her by the spirits of darkness and death.

Romans 10:6-10: ***"But the righteousness which is of faith speaks on this wise, … The word is near you, even in your mouth, and in your heart, that is, the word of faith, which we preach; that if you shall confess with your mouth the Lord Jesus, and shall believe in your heart that God has raised Him from the dead, you shall be saved."*** The key is confessing with the mouth what you believe in your heart. The authority is in your mouth for you to use against the forces of darkness.

The cross, where Jesus bore our shame that we might share in His glory, could have been avoided if Jesus had so desired. He could have called legions of angels to rescue Him and destroy all of His enemies, but He didn't. We have the same right, to call for the Father to dispatch angels to help us in time of need and to watch over us, and all that the Father has given us.

John 6:63: ***"It is the Spirit that quickens (gives life); the flesh profits nothing: the words I speak to you, they are Spirit, and they are life."*** Proverbs 18:21: ***"Death and life are in the power of the tongue: and they that love it shall eat the fruit thereof."*** The power of the words that we speak will either bless or curse someone or some situation. They will produce life or death. Words that are spoken by the leadership of the Holy Spirit produce life and those spoken by our emotions or human reasoning produce death. The Holy Spirit speaks life into our lives and situations because He is speaking the very Word of the Lord. His words are always light and truth: spoken in the love of the Father. They are words designed to bless us and/or others when we are obedient to Him. The words that Jesus spoke were the words of the Father because He said, ***"I speak what I hear My Father saying."*** Jesus spoke the words of the Father into lives and circumstances because they were life to the people and circumstances. Of course, not everything He spoke was a blessing, i.e. He cursed the fig tree and it died. But in the dying of the fig tree, He taught His disciples an important lesson, so even these words became life to those who heard and received them. If Jesus spoke "life" by the Spirit, then we should speak life also. Satan always comes to bring death and destruction but Jesus comes to bring ***"life and that more abundantly"*** when He speaks. We should do likewise. So our admonition here is to be sure that the words we speak are Spirit and life.

John 15:7: ***"If you abide (live in Me—virtually united with) in Me, and My words abide (remain in you and continue to live in your hearts), ask what you will and it shall be done for you."*** (v.8) ***"Herein is My Father glorified, that you bear much fruit; so shall you be My disciples."*** John 1:1: ***"In the beginning was the Word, and the Word was with God and the Word was God."*** God said, and it was. As we remain united in intimate relationship with the Father and Jesus (the Word), we will speak those things that are in our hearts and they will come to pass because we speak The Word, in truth and authority. (He is Truth and the authority is His.) Jesus told His disciples that the Kingdom of God was at hand and He demonstrated to them what it looked like: He healed, delivered, cast out demons, and did many miracles by the power of the Holy Spirit in order to reveal the Lord's desire for the church by giving power to it over the Kingdom of darkness.

It is all about the Kingdom of Heaven and the church is the vehicle through which the Father chose to reveal His power and authority over the kingdom of Darkness and the works of Satan. We are to speak the Word of power and truth into this present world system of darkness, sickness, disease, bondage, fear and many other evil circumstances, that this spoken word, ***"the gates of hell shall not prevail against the***

***church,"*** shall come true. If we are to witness salvation, deliverance, healing, setting free, and peace, then the Word of God should be spoken in power and authority—this is the Kingdom made manifest. It is not about special ministries, individuals, or organizations, but it is about His Kingdom (King Jesus), being made manifest and destroying the works of Satan, in His Name and by His power.

Revelation 12:11: ***"And they overcame him by the blood of the Lamb, and by the word of their testimony; and they loved not their lives to the death."*** The victory over the kingdom of darkness comes "by the blood of the Lamb" but also by our words of testimony of what Jesus has done and His power over Satan and by the fact that they did not love their lives, even if it meant death.

Matthew 12:37: ***"For by your words you shall be justified, and by your words you shall be condemned."*** The words that we speak will bring either justification or condemnation to us.

2 Corinthians 10:4 ***"For the weapons of our warfare are not carnal, but mighty through God to the pulling down of strongholds."*** Our weapons against Satan and the spirits of darkness are not carnal, but spiritual; and our weapons are mighty through God—not carnality. These weapons are for pulling down the strongholds in our lives and setting us free. A stronghold is a thought pattern or imaginations that are not based on God's truth but based on Satan's lies and deception. They are ungodly desires in our minds or hearts that we yield to on a regular basis and usually succumb to easily.

There must come a desire to change and become like our Lord Jesus and allow His mind to rule in ours instead of unholy thoughts and imaginations. We can say, "I appropriate the faith of Jesus for this situation now." The thoughts that we think continually will develop into our character, which we will become—good or bad.

Ephesians 2:5-6: ***"Even when we were dead in sins (God) has quickened us together with Christ, (by grace you are saved) and has raised us up together, and made us sit together in heavenly places in Christ Jesus."***

We have authority, Jesus' authority, because He has raised us up to sit with Him on the right hand of the Father in Heaven. The authority that we speak in against the darkness is not of us but of the One who earned it—Jesus. The Father did not just give the throne, at His right hand, to Jesus because He was His Son, but gave it to Him because as the Son of Man, He earned that right.

Philippians 3:20: "***For our citizenship is in Heaven...***" We are citizens of the Kingdom of Heaven and Christ Jesus is our King. We are under His authority and the words that we speak are to be the words that He speaks about His Kingdom, for His Kingdom is eternal but this earthly kingdom is temporal.

Colossians 1:13: ***"Who (the Father) has delivered us from the power of darkness, and has translated us into the Kingdom of His dear Son:"*** He has *already* delivered us from the power of darkness and, in the spirit, we sit in His Kingdom. We have the right and opportunity to come before the Father, in His dear Son's Name, and ask what we will of Him (that will glorify Him), and He will do it.

Colossians 3:1-3: ***"If you then be risen with Christ, seek those things which are above, where Christ sits on the right hand of God. Set your affection (mind and emotions) on things above, not on things on the earth. For you are dead, and your life is hid with Christ in God."*** If we are risen and sit with Jesus in Heaven, then we should seek those things which are heavenly; namely, allowing Him to speak, touch and live through our vessels of clay (clay so that He might receive *all* of the glory for all deeds done in and through this body). 2 Corinthians 4:7: ***"If our life is hid in Jesus, then others will not see us and not be praising us but will rather give God the glory."***

Romans 16:25: ***"Now to Him that is of power to establish you according to my gospel, and the preaching of Jesus Christ, ...*** " We have been empowered according to the gospel and preaching of Jesus Christ, in His name, to proclaim the Word and promises of God with power.

If we are to ***"live and move and have our being in Christ Jesus"*** (Acts 7:28) with His power made manifest through us then forgiveness will be manifested in our lives. In Matthew 18:21-35, we read what Jesus had to say about forgiveness. He said we will be released to demons to torment us ***"... if you from your hearts forgive not every one his brother their trespasses."***

We have been forgiven and it is imperative that, in the same way, we forgive our brothers who have sinned against us. Our Father cannot and will not receive our prayers if there is sin in our lives, namely not forgiving others.

Jude 9 states, ***"... The Lord rebuke you."*** We can ask God to bless or rebuke someone. We do not rebuke Satan, but the Lord will. We can say, "The Lord rebuke you in Jesus' name, or the Lord bless you in Jesus' name."

When we meet someone, we can say, "It's a fine day and Jesus is Lord." This statement always opens the door for someone to join into a conversation about the Lord.

John 7:17 says, ***"If any man will do His will, he shall know of the doctrine, whether it be of God..."*** If we don't know what to do then, we haven't totally committed to do His will. Jesus said that if we will do His will, then we shall know what His Word says. If we know His will and His Word, then we need to command things to happen just as Jesus did. He spoke to circumstances, sickness, disease, demons, trees, wind, and many other things and they obeyed—because they understood authority—authority that God gave to Jesus, who has in turn given it to us to do likewise.

Ezekiel 28:3 says of Satan, ***"Behold, you are wiser than Daniel; there is no secret that they can hide from you."*** Satan knows our thoughts and there is no secret hid from him. It is therefore necessary that we maintain holy and pure thoughts, with no darkness in our hearts as no open door for Satan to enter into our minds and circumstances.

Proverbs 28:5 states, ***"They that seek the Lord understand all things."*** So, if we want understanding, we need to seek the Lord. Seeking, however, is more than just a passing thought. If you lost something of great value, you would be very diligent in "seeking" to find it. This same type of diligence should be evidenced when we "seek" the Lord.

Hebrews 5:12 addresses the issue of us being able to fulfill the Great Commission which says we are to "go and make disciples" of others. ***"For when for the time you ought to be teachers, you have need that one teach you again which be the first principles of the oracles of God: and are become such as have need of milk, and not strong meat. (v. 14) But strong meat belongs to them that are of full age, even those who by reason of use have their senses trained to discern both good and evil."***

So, speak His word, and know and use Jesus' parables that it might be as Isaiah said, (Is. 42:13 Amp.) ***"The Lord will go forth as a mighty man; He will rouse His zealous indignation and vengeance like a warrior; He will cry, yes, He will shout aloud, He will do mightily against His enemies."***

**It has always been a principle of Servants of the King to never ask for money. We are not requesting it now. However, if you are pleased with the work God is accomplishing through Servants of the King AND if you feel led to contribute to its continuing ministry, please go to www.servantsoftheking.org.**

**There are so many stories from Kemper Crabb's ministry we were not able to include in this book. If your favorite is not included, please forgive the author who endeavored to accomplish Kemper's aim of equipping the Body of Christ to spread the Good News of salvation and the alleviation of suffering.**

**All proceeds from the sale of this book, in their entirety, go to the ongoing ministry of Kemper Crabb and Servants of the King.**

CPSIA information can be obtained
at www.ICGtesting.com
Printed in the USA
LVHW07s0924170718
584007LV00008B/21/P